Design Against Crime

T0300087

Design Against Crime will aid the design profession to meet the challenges presented by the competing needs and complex systems around crime and security. It proposes that designers should use their creative talents to develop innovative solutions to security problems that contribute to the ongoing fight against crime.

The authors first explain the Design Against Crime approach to safety and security. They go on to provide practical advice on addressing crime and insecurity within the design process and offer practical examples of design being applied to safety and security problems. They also examine crime victimisation from a global perspective, highlighting the benefits worldwide of reducing opportunities for crime, including issues of national security, such as terrorism.

A design-led, human-centred approach provides a way forward that is both aspirational and practical. The book is aimed primarily at design professionals, educators and students interested in safety and security, from all design disciplines, including product design, architecture, service design and communication design. The book should also be read by crime prevention experts, planners, local authorities, managers of urban environments and policymakers.

Dr Caroline L. Davey and **Andrew B. Wootton** are founders and Co-Directors of the *Design Against Crime Solution Centre* at the University of Salford, UK.

Caroline is a qualified Organisational Psychologist and Reader in *Design, Innovation & Society* in the School of Arts and Media.

Andrew is an Industrial Designer and is Senior Research Fellow in *Human-Centred Design* in the School of Arts and Media.

Design for Social Responsibility
Series Editor: Rachel Cooper

Social responsibility, in various disguises, has been a recurring theme in design for many years. Since the 1960s several more or less commercial approaches have evolved. In the 1970s designers were encouraged to abandon 'design for profit' in favour of a more compassionate approach inspired by Victor Papanek. In the 1980s and 1990s profit and ethical issues were no longer considered mutually exclusive and more market-oriented concepts emerged, such as the 'green consumer' and ethical investment. The purchase of socially responsible, 'ethical' products and services has been stimulated by the dissemination of research into sustainability issues in consumer publications. Accessibility and inclusivity have also attracted a great deal of design interest and recently designers have turned to solving social and crime-related problems. Organisations supporting and funding such projects have recently included the NHS (research into design for patient safety), the Home Office (Design Against Crime) and Engineering and Physical Sciences Research Council (design decision-making for urban sustainability).

Businesses are encouraged (and increasingly forced by legislation) to set their own socially responsible agendas that depend on design to be realised. Design decisions all have environmental, social and ethical impacts, so there is a pressing need to provide guidelines for designers and design students within an overarching framework that takes a holistic approach to socially responsible design. This edited series of guides is aimed at students of design, product development, architecture and marketing, and design and management professionals working in the sectors covered by each title. Each volume includes: The background and history of the topic, its significance in social and commercial contexts and trends in the field, exemplar design case studies, guidelines for the designer and advice on tools, techniques and resources available.

1 Design for Micro-Utopias
  Making the unthinkable possible
  John Wood

2 Design for Inclusivity
  A practical guide to accessible, innovative and user-centred design
  Roger Coleman, John Clarkson and Julia Cassim

Design Against Crime

A Human-Centred Approach to
Designing for Safety and Security

Caroline L. Davey and
Andrew B. Wootton

Routledge
Taylor & Francis Group

LONDON AND NEW YORK

First published 2017
by Routledge
2 Park Square, Milton Park, Abingdon, Oxon OX14 4RN

and by Routledge
52 Vanderbilt Avenue, New York, NY 10017

First issued in paperback 2020

Routledge is an imprint of the Taylor & Francis Group, an informa business

British Library Cataloguing-in-Publication Data
A catalogue record for this book is available from the British Library

Library of Congress Cataloging-in-Publication Data
A catalog record for this title has been requested

ISBN 13: 978-0-367-66990-4 (pbk)
ISBN 13: 978-0-7546-4501-6 (hbk)

Typeset in Bembo
by Apex CoVantage, LLC

Contents

Figures

Tables

Part I

Introducing Design Against Crime

1 Introduction

It's a common belief that crime occurs everywhere and is somehow inevitable and that there is nothing we can do about it. Such sentiment is reflected in phrases like, 'If they want to get in, then they will' and 'If you make a property more secure, the criminal will simply move elsewhere.' It is assumed that crime is in a sense unavoidable, and that the only hope of preventing crime is through increased 'hard' security measures, such as alarms, CCTV and locks – devices traditionally provided by the security industry.

Design Against Crime

Design Against Crime began as a UK initiative to improve everyday security by embedding crime prevention within design education and professional design practice, the aim being to improve the likelihood of everyday products and places being less vulnerable to crime. Initiated in 1999 by the UK Home Office, Design Council and Department of Trade and Industry, Design Against Crime aims to demonstrate the value to users and to society of adopting a design-led approach to improving security. Why should this be so? Well, a key skill of designers is understanding and gaining insight into the human

---

Security in design terms

The term 'security' may commonly be associated with bomber jacket–clad nightclub bouncers. However, in design terms 'security' is an emotional state experienced by users of designed products, environments and services. It is an aspect of user satisfaction and well-being with which designers need to be concerned. Security, like good design, can go unnoticed, in that it is most apparent when absent. In Germany, the word for security and safety is the same – 'Sicherheit'. When we use the term 'security' in relation to Design Against Crime, we are referring to a sense of safety and secureness.

user. Designers also have the ability to creatively reframe problems – to adopt innovative perspectives on situations – and to develop inventive yet practical solutions. Through the application of these skills to crime issues, designers can potentially improve security without increasing fear of crime (an unfortunate side effect of some traditional security measures), inconveniencing the user or creating unattractive products or environments. Design outcomes are made less vulnerable to crime by incorporating crime prevention into meaningful and effective design thinking and practice – rather than by retrofitting security devices once a problem emerges.

Over the last decade, the role of design in addressing social and societal challenges has been expanded (Burns *et al.*, 2006; www.bfi.org). Design Against Crime is part of a movement to help policymakers, practitioners and industry address the complex social issues related to crime and security.

Tackling crime and antisocial behaviour, improving feelings of security and enhancing urban well-being are priorities for policymakers and citizens. Victims of crime may suffer financial, physical and psychological harms, which can have negative consequences for their quality of life over the long term. As well as impacting the individual, crime and insecurity can also affect communities and the use of public services, such as public transport. Compared to other European countries, UK citizens are particularly concerned about crime. However, most people are unaware – or perhaps simply reluctant to believe – that crime rates are actually falling, and have been in most developed countries since the mid-1990s. This inaccurate public perception presents a challenge to UK policymakers (Duffy *et al.*, 2008).

Identifying, understanding and meeting the sometimes conflicting needs of the diverse range of stakeholders involved in the crime and security problem domain is a real challenge. However, this is a challenge that we believe the design profession is well placed to meet. In the view of criminologist professor Ken Pease,

> Designers are trained to anticipate many things: the needs and desires of users, environmental impacts, ergonomics and so on. It is they who are best placed to anticipate the crime consequences of products and services, and to gain the upper hand in the technological race against crime.
>
> (Pease, 2001, p. 27)

We recognise that the core value of design flows in great part from its ability to adopt a human-centred approach, in which the intrinsic experience of the user is understood in rich and meaningful ways. Such an approach moves beyond ergonomics to embrace a broader user experience, one built from human perceptions, emotions and aspirations. It is an approach invested in developing, through effective design research, robust, holistic understandings of problems, scenarios and contexts. Consequently, the creative abilities of designers, and their engagement in the development of everyday products and places, may result in solutions to crime issues that are far removed from traditional ideas of what constitutes a 'security solution'. Through adoption of a design-led approach, improved security may be envisaged as an intentional side effect of improved convenience for users. For instance centralised locking systems in motor vehicles are both convenient and increase the likelihood that all doors are locked when leaving a vehicle. Well-designed reception areas greatly improve the quality of experience for visitors to a building, while also increasing security for staff and visitors through informal surveillance.

Opportunity causes crime

Criminal activity is fostered by human attitudes, norms and behaviours, and societal changes may therefore impact on types and levels of crime. However, there's no getting away from the fact that, as well as a potential cure, design also plays a role in the problem of insecurity. Crime is strongly linked to the availability of desirable, affordable products that are vulnerable to theft or attack. In the 1990s, portable products were designed and developed to be carried on the person or fitted to vehicles, a practice that makes the product and often the user vulnerable to attack. These types of products – known as 'hot products' – were targeted by criminals, and included personal stereos and DVD players (Clarke, 1999). These hot products have now evolved into digital media players, mobile phones and satnavs.

As the creators of consumer products, and shapers of social norms and environments, the actions of designers clearly impact on crime and insecurity. The very products loved by consumers for their functionality, convenience and aesthetic value are, if globally successful, likely to become targets for criminals.

Designers can actively prevent their designs from being targeted and exploited by criminals, and should not merely rely on others to deal with security issues arising from their work. Far from being passive, intelligent design can directly address crime issues, protecting users from harm and clients from financial loss and helping create a safer, more secure society. In addition, in being considered by the designer, security can be effectively embedded as part of a well-resolved design solution – rather than being 'bolted on' after the event and potentially harming the user experience and the design's success.

Better integration of security within design prevents crime

Significant effort has been expended to reduce the risk of crime within a number of industries. Combined with changes in user behaviour and the efforts of governments, better design has resulted in reduced levels of crime worldwide, reversing a crime boom that began in the 1960s. At that time, consumer products became far more available and desirable. The products were often relatively small and valuable, making their theft both easier and profitable for potential criminals. Changes in workforce demographics meant that breaking into houses to steal such consumer products also became easier. An increase in both women and men going out to work meant homes were often unoccupied during the day. The result was a three- to fourfold increase in crime in the industrialised world – a 'crime epidemic' (Cohen & Felson, 1979).

Improved integration of security within design is credited with reversing the dramatic and sustained rise in crime that occurred from the 1960s to the 1990s, affecting countries across the world to a greater or less degree (Farrell, 2013; van Dijk *et al.*, 2012). For example in the 1990s, the UK and the Netherlands were identified as 'high-crime' countries. However, better design and security of residential dwellings have resulted in common crimes such as burglary being significantly reduced. In contrast, Denmark has experienced a threefold increase in burglary that is attributed largely to a reluctance amongst policymakers, public sector organisations and citizens to introduce security measures to the design of residential dwellings (van Dijk, 2012/13).

In the 1990s, the automobile industry took steps to improve the integration of security within the design of vehicles. Nowadays, considerable effort is expended on making vehicles safe and secure. The security performance of vehicle designs and the products within them is subject to attack testing and performance monitoring to assess their effectiveness. Consumers have access to information on the security design performance of a potential purchase relative to other vehicle models and makes, making this a factor in customer choice. This initiative was mainly driven by the insurance companies, who have been able to reduce their costs by promoting better security through the premiums set for different models. The resulting improvement in car security is credited with a global reduction in theft of and theft from vehicles. Modern vehicle design has made casual car theft (e.g. for 'joyriding') almost impossible and reduced the number of criminals with the capability of stealing a vehicle to a minority (van Dijk *et al.*, 2007; van Dijk, 2012/13).

By making crime more difficult or riskier through good design, some offences have been significantly reduced or even eliminated. For example since the introduction of tamper-proof packaging designs, there have been virtually no reported cases of products being interfered with. Meanwhile, better design of banks, building societies and post offices in England and Wales has resulted in a reduction in armed robberies from over 500 per year in the 1990s to just 69 in 2012 – that's a drop of more than 86 per cent (The Economist, 2013).

History of design-led crime prevention

Of course, improving safety and security using design is not new. The criminologist Paul Ekblom notes that there are numerous historical examples of design being used to improve security – from castle walls and arrow slits to reduce access for enemies armed with weapons, through to the design of coins and postage stamps to prevent forgery. In the 1940s, US researchers began exploring the relationship between the design of the built environment and incidence of crime. In the 1970s, crime prevention through environmental design (CPTED) emerged in the United States as an effort to design out crime from the urban environment, and has been implemented to varying degrees across the world. In the UK, researchers focused on the decision-making process of criminals. This resulted in the 1980s in the opportunity-focused theory situational crime prevention (SCP) (Schneider & Kitchen, 2007). Both CPTED and SCP are based on scientific evidence that reducing criminal opportunities reduces crime. Conceptually, the 'opportunity' is seen as a fundamental causal factor in the occurrence of crime (Felson & Clarke, 1998).

With its focus on shaping perceptions, motivations and behaviours, design can clearly play a role in influencing potential offenders in terms of their assessment of opportunity and risk. Designers are arguably best placed to deal with the concept of security in relation to the products, environments and systems resulting from their work. Despite this, however, the application of design-led crime prevention remains rather fragmented. Design Against Crime seeks to unite a broad range of initiatives to improve security using design. To do this, Design Against Crime seeks to apply critical and creative human-centred 'design thinking' to the challenge of crime and security.

Measuring the crime problem

Over the last two decades, the body of scientific evidence supporting the value of design in crime prevention has grown significantly. We realise that some readers may be sceptical of claims that crime levels have reduced and that the improved integration of design and security is responsible. Such scepticism may stem from a distrust of police crime statistics – or even statistics in general. For example statistics may be perceived as being misrepresented for political ends. In practice, comparing police crime statistics is difficult, especially across different countries. This is because every nation state has developed its own way of measuring crime. Even in a single country, such as the UK, the way in which police crime data is collected has changed over time, making historical comparison problematic.

Reporting of inaccuracies with police data

The Guardian reports that the gold-standard 'national statistics' status was withdrawn from police-recorded crime figures, due to allegations that some figures have been subject to 'a degree of fiddling'. The point is made that the second yardstick, the Crime Survey for England and Wales, dating back to 1981, is 'unaffected by the allegations and has consistently showed a fall in crime since 1995' (Travis, 2014).

Thanks to the efforts of criminologists in the Netherlands, however, we have access to scientific data on crime levels going back to 1989 with which to test claims of a reduction in crime. Information on crime victimisation and security has been collected from surveys conducted across the world with a representative sample of the population. This data allows the measurement of changes in crime levels over time across different geographic locations. Analysed by criminologists, these surveys have identified the causal factors responsible for increasing or decreasing levels of crime. This approach, known as a crime victimisation survey, overcomes the difficulty of relying on police crime data (van Dijk *et al.*, 2007; van Dijk, 2012/13).

The cost of security

While there is much to celebrate, efforts to fight crime have not been without cost to users and wider society. Critics argue that security measures are ugly, generate feelings of insecurity, create 'a fortress society', perpetuate social exclusion and undermine privacy. Unfortunately, there is some truth to these claims. The protection of people and property has grown into a major industry that is dominated by the makers of 'access control' mechanisms and surveillance systems, such as alarms, CCTV and security fencing.

Meanwhile, technological development has required improved security of information and communication technologies (ICT) used for banking and finance. The growth of mobile communication technologies and the Internet as a forum for online shopping, financial services and social networking has brought a range of security issues to the fore. These range from fraud, identity theft and exploitation of vulnerable individuals to terrorism. Such issues have been tackled using tracking and monitoring technologies, generating societal concerns about the impact of security on privacy and democratic accountability.

The security industry is arguably not concerned enough about the wider, qualitative impact on society of such security measures, which can hamper the achievement by designers, developers and policymakers of often equally desirable objectives. These may include citizens' feelings of security, urban well-being, design usability, convenience, attractiveness and social inclusion.

While CPTED approaches attempt to improve security and reduce feelings of insecurity, they may be championed by those from a more security-oriented background. In many countries, including in the UK, CPTED approaches have been promoted and supported by professions that hold security as the prime objective, believing it should be prioritised over all other potentially desirable outcomes. As such, they tend to rely on a relatively narrow range of solutions to security problems.

The challenge for design

While every person would like a life free from crime and insecurity, other aspirations, ideals and quality of life issues are also important. In the UK, particular political importance has traditionally been attached to crime and justice, which have been a priority for governments since the mid-1980s. However, crime and justice are complex issues in both political and practical terms. It is not simply that different people hold different views, but that the same person can also be inconsistent in his or her attitudes (Duffy *et al.*, 2008).

This book aims to help the design profession and those involved in the discipline of design meet the challenges presented by the competing needs and complex systems around crime and security. It proposes that designers should use their creative talents to develop innovative solutions to security problems that contribute to the ongoing fight against crime. The design profession also has a valuable role to play in understanding and developing strategies to address security with public policy and business strategy, as designers are skilled at synthesising information and communicating complex ideas. UK governments clearly face a real challenge demonstrating the effectiveness of public policy due to misperceptions about crime (Duffy *et al.*, 2008).

This book is aimed primarily at design professionals, educators and students interested in safety and security. We have attempted to make the contents relevant to all design disciplines, including product design, architecture, service design and communication design. Many theories about crime prevention and design originate from the United States and the UK. Practical examples and approaches nevertheless come from across Europe.

We anticipate that the book will attract a wider readership comprising crime prevention experts, planners, local authorities, managers of urban environments and policymakers – who we seek to convince of the value of a design-led approach to security.

The first section explains the Design Against Crime approach to safety and security. Chapter 2 explains how the design of everyday products, places and services impacts on the types and levels of offending behaviour. Crime can be an unfortunate by-product of successful design. We suggest that the design profession is responsible for ensuring that users and clients are not victimised as a result of foreseeable vulnerabilities arising from design decisions. As Chapter 3 explains, the Design Against Crime programme was established to embed crime prevention within design education and practice, and promote its capacity to improve quality of life by addressing societal challenges such as crime and security. It encourages designers to 'think thief' – that is to understand and consider the potential crime issues surrounding their design. Through integration into the design process, design solutions can be developed that prevent crime and insecurity, without compromising other desirable objectives.

The second part provides practical advice on addressing crime and insecurity within the design process. Chapter 4 covers the human experience of crime victimisation and feelings of insecurity, and impact on enjoyment of products, places and services. A negative experience may result in the user avoiding the place, product or service, and may also damage well-being and quality of life. The effect of a negative experience may extend beyond the victim, to the family, neighbours and wider community – as illustrated through the diagram of the tangible and intangible costs of crime (Figure 4.1). In instances where safety and security impact on the user and/or client, these issues need to be addressed within the design development process. How this can be achieved is described in Chapter 5. To be able to employ their creative abilities, designers need to be made aware of crime and related social issues from the project's outset and to be able to incorporate safety and security into key activities – including research and consultation, concept generation and design, feasibility testing and design launch. Concept generation and design activities are the focus of Chapter 6, where designers are helped to consider the design from the perspective of the offender – that is to 'think thief'.

The third part covers practical examples of design being applied to security and safety. As explained in Chapter 7, the Design Against Crime programme aimed to engage children and young people, through contributions to the school curriculum, student design competitions and research projects – at both undergraduate and postgraduate levels. In 2009, a creative Design Against Crime process was developed to engage young people at risk of offending in developing innovative solutions to problems. Chapter 8 focuses on the design of the urban environment – an area to benefit from sustained effort in terms of design policy and practice. It outlines steps taken to encourage key stakeholders to address concerns about crime and insecurity, including architects, planners and city centre managers.

In the fourth part, Chapter 9 examines crime victimisation from a global perspective, highlighting the benefits worldwide of reducing opportunities for crime. Chapter 10 notes the current focus on issues of national security, such as terrorism and natural disasters. While design approach has much to contribute in these areas, the focus for policymakers and practitioners should perhaps be elsewhere – on emerging (and re-emerging) crime problems that impact on people's everyday experience and quality of life. We suggest that research into user experience of safety and security is needed, and that the findings should feed into the design of products, services and communications – not just urban design.

This book is timely because the maintenance of reduced crime levels is threatened by cuts in public spending. In addition, changes to public policy risks fostering commitment to security strategies and solutions that impact negatively on society. A design-led, human-centred approach provides a way forward that is both aspirational and practical.

References

Burns, C., Cottam, H., Vanstone, C. and Winhall, J. (2006) 'Transformation Design'. RED Paper 02. UK Design Council. Download from: http://www.designcouncil.org.uk/publications/transformation-design/

Clarke, R.V. (1999) 'Hot Products: Understanding, Anticipating and Reducing Demand for Stolen Goods'. Police Research Series Paper 112. London: Home Office Research, Development and Statistics Directorate.

Cohen, L.E. and Felson, M. (1979) 'Social Change and Crime Rate Trends: A Routine Activity Approach'. *American Sociological Review*, Vol. 44, pp. 588–605.

Duffy, B., Wake, R., Burrows, T. and Bremner, P. (2008) 'Closing the Gap. Crime and Public Perceptions'. London: Ipsos MORI Social Research Institute. Download from: http://

www.ipsos.com/public-affairs/sites/www.ipsos.com.public-affairs/files/documents/closing_the_gaps.pdf

The Economist. (2013) 'The Curious Case of the Fall in Crime', *Leaders, The Economist*, 20th July 2013. Download from: http://www.economist.com/news/leaders/21582004-crime-plunging-rich-world-keep-it-down-governments-should-focus-prevention-not

Farrell, G. (2013) 'Five Tests for a Theory of the Crime Drop'. Paper presented at International Symposium on Environmental Criminology and Crime Analysis (ECCA), Philadelphia, US.

Felson, M. and Clarke, R.V. (1998) 'Opportunity Makes the Thief: Practical Theory for Crime Prevention'. Police Research Paper 98. London: Home Office.

Pease, K. (2001) *Cracking Crime Through Design*. London: Design Council. p. 27.

Schneider, R.H. and Kitchen, T. (2007) *Crime Prevention and the Built Environment*. London and New York: Routledge.

Travis, A. (2014) 'Police Crime Figures Lose Official Status over Claims of Fiddling'. *The Guardian*, Wednesday 15 January 2014. Download from: http://www.theguardian.com/uk-news/2014/jan/15/police-crime-figures-status-claims-fiddling

van Dijk, J. (2012/13) 'The International Crime Victims Survey, in 'Criminology in Europe''. *Newsletter of the European Society of Criminology*, 2012/13, Vol. 11. Download from: www.esc-eurocrim.org

van Dijk, J., Kesteren, J. and Smit, P. (2007) 'Criminal Victimisation in International Perspective. Key findings from the 2004–2005 ICVS and EU ICS'. Den Haag, Netherlands: WODC. Download from: http://www.unicri.it/services/library_documentation/publications/icvs/publications/ICVS2004_05report.pdf

van Dijk, J., Tseloni, A. and Farrell, G. (2012) 'Introduction'. In Jan van Dijk, Andromachi Tseloni and Graham Farrell (eds.) *The International Crime Drop: New Directions in Research*. Houndsmill, Basingstoke: Palgrave Macmillan. pp. 1–8.

2 User as victim

The dark side of design

The design of everyday products, places and services impacts on the types and levels of offending behaviours. Crime can be an unfortunate by-product of successful design – with sought-after products especially likely to attract criminals. As Chapter 2 explains, this might be considered the 'dark side' of design. We suggest that designers have a moral and professional responsibility to acknowledge this dark side and consider the consequences of their actions. The design profession is responsible for ensuring that users and clients are not victimised as a result of foreseeable vulnerabilities arising from design decisions. The idea that crime and insecurity issues can be design considerations and that security can be built into a design is far from new, as the historical examples in Chapter 3 show. An awareness of the potential negative consequences of design may be considered an input of socially responsible design decision-making. As UK criminologist Ken Pease suggests,

> Why should one reduce the opportunities afforded by the everyday world? The obvious answer is to improve the quality of life of those who would otherwise fall victim to it, or live in fear of it. The less obvious answer is that it is surely immoral, to paraphrase the poet John Donne, to be the gateway to another man's sin.
>
> (Pease, 2001, p. 9)

Crime as a by-product of design

Design and crime are linked – this is an unfortunate fact. Research has shown that the development of desirable products like mobile phones has led to increased numbers of victims of robbery, while the growth of portable satellite navigation devices has been linked with increased theft from motor vehicles. In the UK in the 1990s, the increased use of newly designed mobile phones elicited a wave of robberies that made both adult and child users victims of crime (Harrington & Mayhew, 2001).

Successful products purchased by consumers and widely used are attractive to criminals, who seek to steal, copy or counterfeit the products, and sell them. This 'dark side' of design is described in Figure 2.1, which illustrates how the

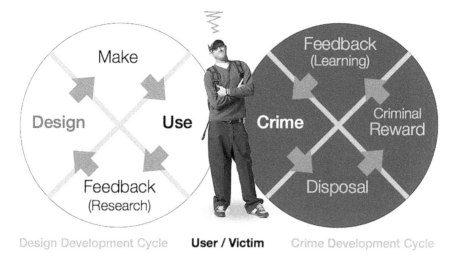

Figure 2.1 The dark side of the design system (the acquisitive crime system).

Source: Davey & Wootton (2012). Material produced to support the development of the UK Design Council Guidelines on Designing Out Crime.

'design system' intersects with the 'crime system' through the user (or victim). Decisions made in the design system impact on the scale and efficiency of the crime system. This is especially true for so-called acquisitive crime, which includes robbery, theft, burglary and vehicle crime.

Too often, the user of the designed product can become a victim of crime. Over multiple incidents, a process for criminal disposal and reward emerges, becoming refined and reinforced so that offenders learn to target design types that fit into this process. Such targeting may be the result of vulnerabilities in the designed item itself, or in the user behaviours that the design engenders. Such targeting behaviour by offenders has been termed a 'crime harvest' and can be attributed to design. The criminologist Ken Pease (2001) explains that design-related crime problems typically follow three phases:

1   Design with indifference to crime consequences
2   The reaping of a 'crime harvest'
3   Retrofitting of security solution (or withdrawal of design).

Retrofitting security solutions to crime problems frequently results in the bolt-ing on of functions or attributes unsympathetic to the original design. For example in the case of the design of the built environment, this may include additional security fencing, barbed wire and CCTV – often at considerably more cost than would have been expended were crime and security effectively considered at the design stage.

For the sake of all stakeholders – users, potential victims, and the organisations and individuals who design new products, services and environments – the best option is to avoid Phase 1 of the process outlined earlier, and design with appropriate consideration of crime and security.

Easy and tempting opportunities

As already discussed, some products are more at risk of crime than others. This is because offenders are choosy about what they steal, tending to focus on items that have high intrinsic value and/or can be easily sold and turned into cash. Like legitimate users, offenders value convenience. As a result, products perceived as being valuable, easy to remove and easy to carry are more likely to be targeted.

Indeed, research into the products targeted by criminals has provided useful insight into offender selection criteria. In 1999, the criminologist Ronald V. Clarke identified the particular characteristics common to products most often targeted (Clarke, 1999). These features were organised to create an acronym to describe such 'hot' products: CRAVED.

> C – Concealable (easily hidden after theft; or theft not likely to be noticed initially)
> R – Removable (easily taken, carried and transported – especially on the person)
> A – Available (on display; or in an insecure location; or not being watched over)
> V – Valuable (of significant monetary value, or signifying status or power)
> E – Enjoyable (fun to use or possess, and therefore desirable)
> D – Disposable (easily sold on or exchanged for cash, drugs, etc.)

Hot products

Cash is the most frequently stolen item in thefts, burglaries and robberies. When viewed through the lens of CRAVED criteria, cash is at the top of the scale, the very hottest of hot products. Its presence or absence determines the location of many types of thefts, from bank robberies through muggings near ATMs to thefts from ticket machines. Clearly, the 'valuable' and 'disposable' aspects of CRAVED inherent in the design of our paper currency system render cash a very attractive target. Changing the design of cash to reduce these factors would likely create expensive problems for its legitimate users. However, designers of systems that include cash need to recognise that it will increase the likelihood of said system being targeted by offenders – and make this a design consideration.

Besides cash, thieves tend to target a relatively small number of hot products, including cars, laptop computers, DVD players, satnavs and mobile phones. Perhaps predictably, the items falling within the hot product category vary depending on both what is available and what is fashionable. In previous years, hot products targeted by thieves have included hi-fi systems, DVD recorders, televisions and other household electronic products. However, as prices of such home entertainment systems have dropped, the pattern of crime has changed. A rise in ownership of 'personal electronic devices', such as iPods, portable games systems and, lately, smartphones, has seen many offenders switching from burglary to mugging as a means of targeting these current hot products (ONS, 2013).

Growth in the manufacture and widespread use of personal electronics – consumer products designed to be carried on the person – has been a source of crime problems since the 1990s. In 2008, the five most stolen electronic devices in the United States were as follows (Switched Staff, 2008):

- iPods
- Laptops
- Mobile phones
- GPS (satnav systems)
- Car stereos.

The designers of such hot products need to bear in mind the role of their design solutions in putting their users at increased risk of victimisation. We would suggest that some responsibility needs to be taken by designers for crime and security issues directly arising from their work. Government initiatives seek to foster industry responsibility for crime waves, and some industries have endeavoured to 'crime proof' everyday products targeted by offenders (Ekblom, 2012).

Environments for crime

Offenders don't only focus on the target but also are selective about *where* they commit crimes. Research suggests that places that are easily accessible, free from surveillance (by CCTV or other users) and easy to damage are most vulnerable to crime. A good deal of research has been undertaken to understand the decisions that they make about offending. This has led to the development of what has been termed the 'rational choice' perspective to understand offender decision-making (Clarke & Felson, 1993). This approach posits that offenders make decisions based on their understanding of a given situation in terms of perceived benefits and costs. Such understandings may include, for example, the risk of being seen (a cost), or the knowledge that a particular product they have spotted can be easily sold (a benefit). Such decisions are called 'rational' in that they are considered and any actions resulting are purposeful.

In many ways, attempts by criminologists to understand criminal behaviour are comparable to design research into user behaviour. Both seek to understand motives and the cognitive drivers that underpin decision-making. For offenders, there are four main questions they ask themselves just before committing an offence (Design Council, 2003, p. 22):

1   Can I be seen?
2   If I am seen, will I be noticed?
3   If I am seen and noticed, will anybody do anything about it?
4   Can my escape route be sabotaged?

Designing in features that are likely to make the prospective offender answer 'yes' to any of these questions has the potential to prevent a crime occurring. Opportunities for crime can be envisaged as having three components, as shown in Figure 2.2.

These three components form what is known as the *basic crime triangle* (Felson, 1998, cited in Felson & Clarke, 1998):

1   *A likely offender* – Someone who is more likely than not to take advantage of a criminal opportunity. This may be due to, for example, previous criminal history (e.g. a repeat offender) or personal circumstances at the time (e.g. a drug user needing to fund a habit). This might also be a person with poor impulse control, such as someone prone to violence.

2   *Suitable target* – For example a product that falls into the CRAVED category discussed earlier, or something that will provide an outlet for whatever the potential offender happens to be seeking (e.g. a bus shelter to damage, a rubbish bin to set on fire).

3   *The absence of a capable guardian* – A 'capable guardian' is someone who the offender perceives might potentially intervene in the offence. They could either prevent the offence happening or identify, report and even apprehend the offender. A capable guardian can be formal (e.g. a police officer or security guard) or informal (e.g. a mindful owner, or simply a passerby). If the offender perceives that there is no one acting in this capable guardian role in a particular situation, the offender will be more likely to commit the offence.

Figure 2.2 The three components of the crime triangle.

Source: *Opportunity Makes the Thief. Practical Theory for Crime Prevention. Police Research Series Paper 98.* London: Home Office, Policing and Reducing Crime Unit, Research, Development and Statistics Directorate.

Design decisions can inadvertently generate opportunities for crime by enabling potential offenders to be present in a situation where an opportunity for crime exists. This is usually caused by a change in user behaviour, which might be down to the design of an environment or equally the design of a product or service. For example the introduction of through routes to a residential area can impact negatively on the security of users and residents, as these may become shortcuts used by offenders and provide an opportunity to scope potential targets. Similarly, the design of mobile phones has led to users leaving their phones easily accessible on tables in restaurants and bars, and increased the availability of opportunities for theft. In terms of service design, there is some evidence that the rise in self-service checkouts at supermarkets has led to a rise in opportunistic theft. A recent survey of nearly 5,000 people by British consumer website watch-mywallet.co.uk found that nearly a third of shoppers have admitted to stealing from grocery stores while using self-service checkout lanes (O'Meara, 2013).

Offenders also make use of design features of the environment to commit crime – for example using architectural features or items of street furniture to scale a property's perimeter, wheely bins to transport stolen goods and materials from unsecured building sites to carry out acts of vandalism.

Behaviours motivated by emotion – rather than a purposeful intention to steal – are also strongly influenced by environmental design. Alcohol consumption can result in feelings of aggression, with aggressive behaviour breaking out in situations where the potential for conflict is high. Situational factors likely to foster outbreaks of aggressive behaviour include: overcrowded venues; busy bar areas; cluttered seating areas; and queues at public transport stops and taxi ranks. Design can impact on the consequences of aggressive behaviour for both the victim and the offender. A beer glass made from toughened or laminated safety glass is considerably less dangerous if used as a weapon than one made from normal glass. Traditional beer glasses can inflict severe injuries, often resulting in permanent scarring and disfigurement. The thoughtful design of venues, environments, products and systems can help prevent conflict situations from arising, reduce the potential for escalation and minimise physical and psychological harm.

Crime hotspots

Designers who develop services and buildings for use in high-crime locations have a particular responsibility for crime prevention. Crime tends to be concentrated along particular routes or around particular locations, sometimes identified by police as 'crime hotspots'. Offenders observe and seize opportunities for crime as they go about their daily activities – travelling to meet friends, visiting shops and so on. As a result, crime is often prevalent along routes to frequently used facilities, such as schools, parks and recreation centres, shopping areas and transport services.

In addition, motivated offenders will seek out environments that provide opportunities for crime – especially if such locations support their preferred offending behaviour. For example pickpockets are attracted to crowded locations where they can pass unnoticed and where legitimate users carry valuables, such as city centres and transport interchanges. Train stations are a focus for crime problems across a wide range of urban and national contexts, precisely because they bring together potential offenders and suitable targets. When reviewing the level of crime in a city, often the largest hotspot is around the main train station.

Users vulnerable to crime

Some users groups are particularly vulnerable to crime, and designers need to understand the particular risks and take steps to prevent them becoming victims. For example students in higher education institutions are a victimised group, being twice as likely as any other group to be victims of theft. Home Office research suggests one in three fall victim to crime while at university (NUS, 2009). Students are often targeted by criminals during the first few weeks of term – about 20 per cent of student robberies occur in the first six weeks of the academic year. It is estimated that a third of all students become victims of crime, mainly theft and burglary (Complete University Guide, 2013).

While older people may be more worried about crime, young people are actually at greater risk of becoming victims. Young men are more often victimised than young women, but the growing use of mobile electronic products in the last decade has actually increased the targeting of young women for robbery. The results of the 2011/12 Crime Survey for England and Wales show that victims of mobile phone theft were most likely to be children or young adults aged 14 to 24 years, with victimisation being twice the average rate. In fact it is women aged 18 to 24 who are at highest risk of becoming victim to mobile phone theft, with 1 in 20 experiencing a theft over the last 12 months (ONS, 2013). Security is a major concern for women and parents, and these user groups may modify their behaviour (e.g. avoid using mobile phones in public places), switch to models that are less vulnerable to crime or reconsider whether to purchase a phone for children at all.

Designing for criminal careers

Offenders are tempted by items that are of value, and are more likely to offend if easy opportunities come their way. Consequently, designs that are widely used but vulnerable to crime may not only cause crime levels to increase but also breed a new generation of offenders.

Criminologist Ken Pease cites the 1980s Ford Cortina motor car as an example of design's role in creating offenders (2001, p. 7). In the 1980s, the Ford Cortina became the target of offenders who took cars without permission – what was termed by the media as 'joyriding'. Police crime prevention officers estimated that anyone with a Cortina key had a 50 per cent chance of being able to open any other Cortina with the same key. Poor design of basic car security helped create record numbers of young offenders, who when caught not only were detained at taxpayer expense but also risked being diverted into a life of crime. Research indicates that offenders whose first offence – termed by the police their 'debut' offence – is either vehicle theft, robbery or burglary are most likely to become long-term, repeat offenders (Owen & Cooper, 2013).

We would suggest that designers' professional role includes a wider responsibility to society for the role that their design decisions play in creating (and potentially prolonging) criminal careers.

The cost of crime prevention

Designers may be reluctant to consider crime issues in their work due to concern that addressing crime will inevitably be costly. However, this is not the case. Designers are in fact best placed to address crime and security cost-effectively, as such issues can be considered at little additional cost in the early stages of the design project.

When working on a project, designers already have to understand and consider a wide range of issues. What is required is that relevant crime risks and issues are identified during the initial 'set-up' phase of the project. This may involve consulting with suitable experts (e.g. police and crime prevention specialists) and reviewing sources of information on crime, security and design. If one or more specific crime and security issue is identified, then this can be explored in more detail by the design team during the early stage of the project, when other design research is conducted and ideas generated. Other project team members may also provide input to the process, through, for example, market research, or provision of customer feedback about existing products.

During the idea generation phase, designers develop a range of concepts, evaluating them against customer needs and the project requirements. The costs and benefits of the design solution will be considered in some detail when selecting a design concept to take forward. Design solutions that address crime and security issues will not necessarily be more expensive, and may indeed prove less costly over the longer term of the entire product life cycle. For instance the location and design of customer toilets should be carefully considered to reduce the potential for illegal activities, such as drug dealing and vandalism. When entrances to toilets are easily overlooked by staff, the need to employ additional security staff may be reduced or eliminated.

The risk of crime can be reduced in some cases simply by considering and modifying management or staff practices. Theft from retail premises has been shown to decrease simply by shop assistants greeting customers on entering the premises. This reduces the sense of anonymity felt by individuals entering who might consider shoplifting, and so increases their perception of risk.

In 2000, the criminologist Rachel Armitage evaluated the cost and effectiveness of making residential housing in West Yorkshire more secure. Her research compared houses built or refurnished to designs conforming to the

UK police security standard 'Secured by Design' (SBD). Using figures provided by registered social landlords, surveyors and builders, she calculated that it cost on average an extra £440 to make residential dwellings more secure at the development stage. Where existing homes were refurbished to the SBD standard, the costs rose to approximately £600 per dwelling. In other words, it costs about a third more to implement good security after a dwelling is built, demonstrating the cost benefit of addressing security at the design stage. The benefits of design modifications to reduce crime have been proven to outweigh the costs (Welsh & Farrington, 1999).

Client buy-in

While designers may arguably have a moral and professional obligation to consider the risk of crime and security issues arising from their work, they do not generally undertake such work for themselves. Designers are usually contracted by clients – many of whom may feel no such obligation to consider such issues. Understanding the values and perceptions of the client and meeting the client's needs and requirements are fundamental to a designer's commercial success. The client pays the designer for his or her work, and bases decisions about whether to employ the designer in the future on the quality and cost of previous work. Furthermore, the focus and priorities of a design project are generally set by the client, who will have his or her own expectations for the enterprise, which the designer has to understand, manage and accommodate. Some designers are employed by a firm on a longer-term basis, rather than being contracted by a client for specific projects. But such 'in-house' designers certainly don't have free rein. In-house designers must take into account company and senior management objectives and expectations. So, why might designers' external or internal clients be interested in addressing crime and security issues?

There are three main risks for the client in relation to not considering security and crime prevention in the design of a product, service or environment – all of which potentially impact on the company's bottom line:

- The design is targeted by offenders.
- The design is misused for ill.
- The design causes harm.

Design targeted by offenders

Products, services and environments can become targets for criminals, potentially putting users, customer service staff and security staff at risk. This can lead to customer dissatisfaction, negative publicity, government intervention or customer boycotts.

Security issues have been addressed by retail banks because the sector was concerned about the trauma for staff and clients who witnessed an armed robbery and about bad publicity from such high-profile incidents (Reilly *et al.*, 2012). Post offices have also taken steps to protect employees from the trauma of armed robbery.

Mobile phone companies have been pressured by the UK government to address the problem of robbery created by the widespread use of mobile phones attractive to criminals. The Mobile Industry Crime Action Forum launched a charter at the end of 2006, where the majority of mobile phones would be blocked – and hence unusable – within 48 hours of being reported stolen (ONS, 2013).

Protection of personal data and breaches of security are issues for a whole range of organisations, including banks, public service providers and social networking (McIntyre, 2012).

Product misuse

It is possible that designed products or services may be used to commit or assist in criminal offences. For example wheely bins are used by burglars to scale fences and buildings, and to transport goods stolen from houses and building sites. Beer glasses can be employed as weapons during arguments and fights in bars and clubs, causing terrible facial injuries. The misuse of a company's product or service can result in customers switching to alternatives considered 'safer' or incurring less risk. For example safer beer glasses have been developed and sold to licensed premises that suffer from high levels of violence in the busy late-night economy.

Product harm

In some industries, the potential harm caused by products is well documented and additional efforts have to be made to counter these affects. Alcohol, for example, if consumed irresponsibly, is linked to a range of social and health problems. As a result, the industry has taken a number of measures to reduce the impact of this risk on their business model.

The business of alcohol responsibility

The beverage alcohol industry's social responsibility activities can best be described in two parts. First, there are activities that pertain to alcohol use itself. Beverage alcohol, when consumed responsibly, can be part of a balanced, healthy lifestyle; but when consumed inappropriately, it has the potential for serious harm. This has led members of the beverage alcohol industry, especially within the past decade, to form separate organisations – social aspects organisations (SAOs) – whose sole function is to promote responsible drinking. The second part of the industry's corporate responsibility activities relates to the bigger picture. The beverage alcohol industry recognises that good corporate citizenship is more than ensuring that its products are used safely and responsibly. It also entails balancing the needs of its employees for a safe and rewarding job, improving the environment in which they work, and positively engaging the wider culture in which they operate, with the needs of shareholders for a fair return on investment.

Source: International Center for Alcohol policies: www.icap.org/AboutICAP/Policy Approach/Partnerships/CorporateSocialResponsibilityCSR/tabid/190/Default. aspx

Client benefits

Since security is an issue for customers and other stakeholders, there are potential business benefits for clients who take steps to address the risks. Such steps will contribute to a company's corporate social responsibility (CSR) strategy. A model illustrating the benefits for the client of considering security and crime prevention in relation to six business stakeholder groups is shown in Figure 2.3.

Government – promotes regulatory leniency and support

Products and services sometime cause crime waves or generate additional problems for the police (e.g. bars and clubs generate crime and antisocial behaviour on Friday and Saturday nights). Designers, manufacturers and retailers are often then criticised by governments, customers and the general public for being socially irresponsible, thereby increasing the likelihood that companies will be expected to pay for crime resulting from their activities. This is based on the principle of the 'polluter pays'. Local and national government is increasingly looking to business to pay for crime associated with its services, places or products – particularly in industries benefiting from high profits. Bar owners and football clubs are already contributing to policing costs, and developers in Greater Manchester are paying for building plans to be assessed in terms of vulnerability to crime (Davey & Wootton, 2015; www. designforsecurity.org). Private companies want to avoid such criticism, and may wish to demonstrate their commitment to social issues by developing policies related to CSR or sustainability.

Customers and users – encourages custom, loyalty and endorsement

People want to feel good about the brands they purchase, buy from and work with. Some new products and services have become associated with antisocial behaviour and/or crime (e.g. alco-pops linked to binge drinking and large oil companies accused of harming employees and local people in the developing world). This can result in the company being perceived as 'irresponsible' or

Figure 2.3 Business benefits of addressing security as part of a CSR approach.
Source: Davey & Wootton (2006).

'unethical', deterring customers from purchasing its products and, in some cases, prompting customer boycotts. In some industries, customers expect their security to be considered (e.g. the car industry, where many security measures have become standard). Security features may be considered a sales feature, in some instances.

Business networks – gains positive publicity and support

Many companies work together through business networks to address issues of CSR (e.g. Business in the Community). Efforts to address security issues can be shared through business networks, and may, in turn, generate positive publicity.

Community – encourages acceptance and support from the community

Community support and acceptance are important for companies operating within a whole range of sectors, including construction, health and local government. A company's willingness to address security issues can help to engage community organisations and engender community support and acceptance.

Wider public – engenders positive perceptions

Companies work hard to promote a positive image and to protect their reputations. Companies wish to avoid being associated with negative publicity (e.g. branded sports goods and sweatshops in the 1990s) or being featured in communication campaigns warning customers of the dangers of a particular product or service.

Media – attracts positive publicity

Ideally, companies want to be the subject of positive reports in the media. Steps to address social issues such as crime and antisocial behaviour can be communicated to the media to create positive feeling in the market. An example of this is the design projects publicised by the Design Council as part of its Design Out Crime Initiative, working with a number of design firms (Design Council, 2011; www.designcouncil.org.uk).

Business in the Community network

Business in the Community (BITC) identifies ten 'marketplace responsibility principles', some of which relate to security and crime prevention.

- Manage social and environmental impact of product use
- Support vulnerable customers
- Seek potential customers within excluded groups

Source: BITC (2008). The Marketplace Responsibility Principles. Business in the Community, London. http://www.bitc.org.uk/system/files/4292_marketplace_respons.pdf

---

Tackling the dark side of design

The role of design in generating crime problems is clear. However, designers may be concerned about the impact on their designs of addressing such issues. The next chapter argues that designs can be made less vulnerable to crime, without reducing the value of the design to the user. Indeed, this is the advantage of a Design Against Crime approach that seeks to achieve multiple, desirable outcomes.

References

Armitage, R. (2000) 'An Evaluation of Secured by Design Housing Within West Yorkshire'. Home Office Briefing Note, 7/00.

Clarke, R.V. (1999) 'Hot Products: Understanding, Anticipating and Reducing Demand for Stolen Goods'. Police Research Series Paper 112. London: Home Office Research, Development and Statistics Directorate.

Clarke, R.V. and Felson, M. (eds.) (1993) *Routine Activity and Rational Choice*. London: Transaction.

Complete University Guide. (2013) 'Complete University Guide Reveals the Best and Worst Cities for Student-Related Crimes'. Download from: http://www.thecomplete universityguide.co.uk/news/the-best-and-worst-cities-for-student-related-crimes/ (accessed 30.01.2014).

Davey, C.L. and Wootton, A.B. (2006) *Mix Matters: Guidelines Enabling Contractors, Consultants & Suppliers to Address Equality & Diversity*. Salford, UK: University of Salford.

Davey, C.L. and Wootton, A.B. (2015) 'Design for Security in Greater Manchester: Entwicklung eines Dienstes zur Integration von Kriminalitätsprävention in Urban Design und Stadtplanung'. In H. Floeting (ed.), *Sicherheit in der Stadt: Rahmenbedingungen – Praxisbeispiele – Internationale Erfahrungen*. Berlin: Deutsches Institut für Urbanistik (DIFU). Download from: https://difu.de/publikationen/2015/sicherheit-in-der-stadt.html

Design Council. (2003) *Think Thief: A Designer's Guide to Designing Out Crime*. London: UK Design Council.

Design Council. (2011) *Designing Out Crime: A Designer's Guide*. London: UK Design Council. Original research conducted by the Design Against Crime Solution Centre, University of Salford. Download from: http://www.designcouncil.org.uk/Documents/Documents/OurWork/Crime/designersGuide_digital.pdf

Ekblom, P. (2012) *Design Against Crime: Crime Proofing Everyday Products*. London: Lynne Rienner.

Felson, M. (1998) *Crime and Everyday Life*. Second edn, Thousand Oaks, CA. Fine Forge Press. Cited in Felson, M. and Clarke, R.V. (1998) 'Opportunity Makes the Thief. Practical Theory for Crime Prevention'. Police Research Series, Paper 98. London: Home Office.

Felson, M. and Clarke, R.V. (1998) 'Opportunity Makes the Thief: Practical Theory for Crime Prevention'. Police Research Series, Paper 98. London: Home Office.

Harrington, V. and Mayhew, P. (2001) 'Mobile Phone Theft: Home Office Research Study'. Home Office Development and Practice Report No. 17. London: Home Office.

McIntyre, S. (2012) 'Which Smartphone Is the Most Secure?' CSO Online – Security and Risk. 5 November. Download from: http://www.csoonline.com/article/691219/which-smartphone-is-the-most-secure-?source=csoartcso (accessed 29.01.2014).

National Union of Students. (2009) 'Social Policy Briefing: Students and Crime Victimisation – Seasonality and Burglary'. SPB/10/30, 30 October 2009. Download from: http://www.nusconnect.org.uk/pageassets/campaigns/welfare/social-policy-briefings/spb-crime-and-seasonality.pdf

O'Meara, S. (2013) '30% of Shoppers Admit to Stealing When Using Self Service Tills'. Watch My Wallet website. 25 March. Download from: http://www.watchmywallet.co.uk/shopping/food-drink/2012/june-(1)/30-of-shoppers-admit-to-stealing-when-using-self-service-tills/

ONS. (2013) 'Chapter 2. Mobile Phone Theft: England and Wales'. London: Office for National Statistics. Download from: http://www.ons.gov.uk/ons/dcp171776_309652.pdf

Owen, N. and Cooper, C. (2013) 'The Start of a Criminal Career: Does the Type of Debut Offence Predict Future Offending?' UK Home Office Research Report 77. November.

Pease, K. (2001) *Cracking Crime Through Design*. London: Design Council.

Reilly, B., Rickman, N. and Witt, R. (2012) 'Robbing Banks. Crime Does Pay – But Not Very Much'. *The Royal Statistical Society*, June. Download from: http://armedrobberyadvice. files.wordpress.com/2012/12/j-1740–9713–2012–00570-x.pdf

Switched Staff (2008) '5 Most Stolen Gadgets'. 31 January 2008. Downloaded from: http:// www.switched.com/2008/01/31/five-most-stolen-gadgets-2/

Welsh, B.C. and Farrington, D. P. (1999) 'Value for Money? A Review of the Costs and Benefits of Situational Crime Prevention'. *The British Journal of Criminology*, Vol. 39, pp. 345–368. Download abstract from: http://bjc.oxfordjournals.org/content/39/3/345. abstract

Websites

Design for Security, Greater Manchester Police. Download from: www.designforsecurity. org (accessed 14.02.14).

UK Design Council, Designing Out Crime, www.designcouncil.org. 'Projects to Design Out Crime Have Been Archived in the Knowledge and Resources Section'. Download from: http://www.designcouncil.org.uk/knowledge-resources

Examples include:

- The Ultimate Pint Glass. Download from: http://www.designcouncil.org.uk/knowledge-resources/ultimate-pint-glass
- Accident & Emergency Design Challenge Evaluation – AE designed to reduce problem of aggression. Download from: http://www.designcouncil.org.uk/knowledge-resources/ae-design-challenge-impact-evaluation

3   What is Design Against Crime?

As we have seen, there is a dark side to the business of design that has the potential to create opportunities for offenders and thereby create victims. However, designers are not merely passive bystanders, but can play an important role in preventing crime. As this chapter will demonstrate, key design skills and competences can enable crime and insecurity to be addressed effectively, without undermining other objectives important to clients, users and wider society, such as convenience, functionality and style. In recognition of the significant role of design in tackling crime, the Design Against Crime programme was established in 1999. Led by the UK Design Council and Home Office, Design Against Crime seeks to embed crime prevention within design education and practice, and promote its capacity to improve quality of life by addressing societal challenges such as crime and security. Design Against Crime encourages designers to 'think thief' – that is to understand and consider the potential crime issues surrounding their design. Security is best achieved by considering crime risk at an early stage in a development project, and consideration of crime issues should ideally be integrated within the design process. This helps to ensure that resulting design solutions address potential crime issues, but are also convenient, attractive and meet other project requirements.

Historical background

Of course, using design to improve security is not new. The benefits of good design to making environments and products safer have been recognised for hundreds of years. In his Royal Society of Arts lecture, 'Less Crime, by Design', Paul Ekblom (2000) highlights a number of historical examples of intelligent design being used to prevent crime, from the building of castles and fortifications to the design of coins and stamps.

For example the milled edge on coins was originally developed to combat the problem of coin clipping, when coins were made from precious metals, such as silver or gold. In the fifteenth century, coins produced by hammering silver were shaved or clipped to almost half of their minted weight, as the stolen metal could be reused or sold. The introduction of the milled edge made it obvious when a coin had been shaved or clipped, increasing the chance of the offender getting caught and effectively removing the opportunity for this crime.

Designing against crime played a role in the replacement of the Penny Black postage stamp with the Penny Red. Penny Black stamps, due to their colour, were franked with red ink to prevent their reuse. Unfortunately, this red ink was water-soluble, which meant that the stamps could be washed and reused. The Penny Red was introduced to allow franking with black ink that was not water-soluble and could not be removed, preventing their illegal reuse. The Design Against Crime programme seeks to raise the consideration of crime and security issues that impact on everyday life to be part of the remit of modern design.

The Design Against Crime programme

Crime and security are generally considered outside of a designer's scope and competence – with responsibility falling to organisations with a clear crime prevention role, such as police and security firms. Design Against Crime seeks to raise awareness amongst designers of their role in crime prevention, and provide practical guidance and examples to support them in their efforts to understand and improve security. By effectively preventing crime, designers protect users from harm and clients from financial loss and help create a safer, more secure society.

Timeline

1999 to 2001: Design Against Crime began in 1999 as a programme of UK Design Council work funded through the Home Office Crime Reduction Programme and developed in partnership with the Department of Trade and Industry. The research was conducted by the University of Salford, Sheffield Hallam and Judge Institute of Management Studies.

In 2001, the UK criminologist Ken Pease wrote the Design Council policy document 'Cracking Crime Through Design'. This policy paper is one of a series which aims to show how design can deliver solutions to issues of concern to society.

2001 to 2003: The Home Office later funded the Design Council to develop a range of activities and resources to raise awareness of crime issues amongst design professionals and in education. Salford and Sheffield came together to form the Design Policy Partnership, which was commissioned to develop design resources and activities, including case studies, teaching materials, a design competition and a professional development programme. The aim was to embed crime prevention within design education and practice, leading to everyday products and places becoming less vulnerable to crime.

In 2003, *Think Thief: A Designer's Guide to Designing Out Crime* was published by the Design Council. *Think Thief* revealed the 'double-life' of objects and places that are employed by offenders to commit crime. It explained the role for designers in preventing crime, and limitations of alternative approaches. Practical examples of design solutions from a range of disciplines were published by the Design Council in the form of an 'Evidence Pack'.

In addition, the Design Council initiated a series of complementary activities on the Design Against Crime theme, including a retail project and a teaching package on theft of personal products, delivered by Central Saint Martins College of Art & Design.

2007 onwards: In 2007, the UK Home Office established the Design & Technology Alliance Against Crime. The Alliance is a group of independent experts from design, industry and law enforcement, tasked with bringing about innovation and encouraging others to 'think crime' in the first stages of design, planning and product development process.

In the project 'Design Out Crime', designers were commissioned to tackle a range of social problems, including alcohol-related violence and bullying in schools. Designers collaborated with manufacturers and technology and materials experts to create more secure mobile phones, a safer pint glass and innovative solutions to crime in schools, related to businesses and at home.

A second guidance document was researched, and was published by the Design Council in 2011 called *Designing Out Crime: A Designers' Guide.* This practical guide gives design practitioners, clients, educators and students information about how the design of products, services and communications can help to prevent crimes occurring, lessen their impact, aid the recovery of stolen items or help apprehend offenders.

The Alliance highlights the benefits to private and public sector organisations of employing designers, arguing that crime should be tackled as part of their commitment to CSR. The Design Council continues to highlight the positive contribution that the design profession can make to tackling 'grand societal challenges' such as crime and security.

Design Against Crime principles

Think thief!

Designers are renowned for focusing on the user – including their emotions, behaviours, attitudes and perceptions. Due to the potential for designs to be misused or abused, Design Against Crime argues that designers' consideration must extend beyond the user, to include also the potential abuser or misuser. To achieve this, designers must learn to 'think thief' – to understand potential offenders' motivations, anticipate their actions and understand the tools, knowledge and skills they employ. To this end, they should not only user-test their concepts but also misuser-test them, incorporating attack testing into their design process. Of course, it's a question not just of thinking 'thief' but also of considering the range of criminal activity relevant to the design project being undertaken (Ekblom, 2012).

The aim is to out-think the offender and develop design solutions that 'short-circuit' potential offenders' behaviour. Importantly, however, this must be achieved without reducing the value of the design solution to legitimate users, increasing fear of crime, creating social problems, or causing the seriousness of the crime to escalate.

Human–centred approach

Techniques like user-centred design (UCD), human-centred design (HCD) and empathic design all draw on the fundamental principle at the heart of good design: the primacy of the human user – his or her needs, desires, capabilities, weaknesses and aspirations.

Design-led crime prevention fosters a 'human-centred' approach to crime prevention and security. Human-centred design focuses on the roles, requirements, abilities and perceptions of *all* the humans in the problem domain being examined. The emphasis is on human agency in any design system, with the objective being to enhance human abilities, overcome human limitations and foster user acceptance (Rouse, 1991). This means that designers consider the offenders and introduce measures to prevent crime, but never lose sight of the user. The user takes priority, and his or her needs and requirements are considered in the fullest sense.

Innovative security solutions

> 'There is no doubt that creativity is the most important human resource of all. Without creativity, there would be no progress, and we would be forever repeating the same patterns.'
>
> −Edward De Bono, 1992, p. 169

Creativity is a highly valued commodity. Many professional designers strive to develop award-winning, original products, services, buildings and environments. There is a fear that 'standard' solutions will undermine their efforts to be original and creative. In relation to the design of the built environment, there are some standard approaches to improving security – preventing access to the back of the property, strengthening doors, paying particular attention to the quality of locks and windows and so on. However, an appropriate design and layout depend on the context – whether the development is in a city centre or entirely suburban, whether on a busy through route or a residential side road. Designers drawing on current good practice for inspiration should therefore consider the appropriateness of the solution to their problem and adapt it as required for the specific context.

The ability to develop new, innovative ways of improving security is valuable – potentially setting designers apart from others in the field of security. Uniformity is not desirable from an aesthetic or crime prevention perspective. Effective crime prevention requires ongoing innovation to outsmart the offender, as criminals are always developing new methods and seeking fresh opportunities.

Innovation does, however, require additional effort and skill, and does introduce an element of risk. Greater attention to developing and testing design solutions is therefore required.

Holistic approach

Holistic design considers the product, place or environment being designed as part of a larger, interconnected system. Such a design approach seeks to fulfil a range of criteria, including aesthetics and suitability to the context, but widening to include sustainability and adaptability to future needs and requirements. A holistic approach to crime prevention is required because design solutions must be integrated within an existing context without undermining other attributes and qualities. In addition, the prevention of crime is most often achieved through a design modification to an existing system, making a holistic understanding of the system critical to design success. Such an understanding will include physical and functional issues, but also intangibles, such as how a space makes the user feel and the messages it communicates to others. We suggest that a holistic, systems-thinking approach to design is fundamental to the delivery of effective crime prevention.

Embedding crime prevention within design

There are several benefits to embedding crime prevention within the early stages of the design process. Designers are better able to understand crime and security issues within the context of all needs and requirements, and so use their creative skills to generate solutions that are better integrated within the overall design solution. Early-stage integration is much preferable to 'retrofitting' unsympathetic security devices after the design is complete, and also cheaper. Whether crime prevention should be integrated within the design process depends on the level of crime risk, as well as the needs and requirements of key stakeholders. The designer has an important role to play in raising the issue of crime and security, but usually does not control the design agenda – so client buy-in is essential (Wootton & Davey, 2012).

The benefit of a design-led approach

Some designers appear reluctant to incorporate crime prevention into design, perhaps fearing that other design features will be compromised. Failure to fulfil the needs of users for convenience, style and so on potentially undermines the potential success of a product. Indeed, designers are expected to achieve multiple objectives, with security being achieved alongside other outcomes desired by users and clients. The extent to which security should be prioritised depends upon a range of factors, including a client's priorities, user needs and user context. The ability to achieve multiple objectives – convenience, style and security – is what sets the design profession apart from the security industry. There are examples of designs where security has been achieved without compromising other desired objectives. Some of these are highlighted ahead.

Secure and convenient

In our experience, designers often equate security with user inconvenience and 'a right pain'. Unfortunately, there is some truth to this. Typical annoyances include carrying bulky locks for bikes, retaining multiple passwords that are soon forgotten, remembering to set domestic alarms, taking your satnav with you when you leave your car, entering a PIN number before you can use your phone and so on. Of course, security and convenience are not necessarily mutually exclusive. For example centralised locking in cars is both convenient and useful from a crime prevention point of view – careless drivers are less likely to leave doors unlocked. As another example, the 'cashback' service offered at supermarket checkouts reduces the amount of cash being held in the till, thereby reducing the risk of theft for the supermarket. However, the service also offers customers the convenience of accessing their cash without having to visit an ATM. As a bonus, withdrawing money via cashback at a supermarket is less risky for the customer than using an ATM. Another convergence of security and convenience can be seen in Apple's recent introduction of fingerprint recognition as a way to both secure and intuitively unlock a smartphone that may these days contain a great deal of sensitive data.

Crime prevention measures that place a heavy burden on the user are often ineffective. For example individuals soon tire of remembering to carry an attack alarm, using different passwords when shopping online, and locking windows. By focusing on user habits and behaviours, designers are well placed to develop security solutions that are suited to their needs and requirements.

Secure and attractive

There is an assumption that additional security will make a design unattractive. This belief is reinforced by the fact that buildings in high-crime areas are often disfigured by defensive 'security' measures, such as razor wire, roller shutters, security grilles, window bars, unsightly types of fencing or even bricked-up windows. The use of such hard security measures often results from crime problems emerging and security measures being retrofitted. In other words, hard and unattractive security measures often result from failure to consider crime during the design stage. Designers are well placed to address security issues without compromising style.

A good example of well-considered security design is the £31 million Experian Data Centre in Nottingham, designed by architects and urban designers Sheppard Robson. Resilience is part of the Experian brand, and the nature of the data centre's business meant that security was a key criterion in the design brief. However, the need to prevent offender access to the site was solved in a particularly innovative way.

Rather than simply surrounding the centre with tall security fencing and ignoring the resulting visual impact this would have, the designers chose a more subtle and creative approach – but without compromising security. A reed bed was designed along the length of the iconic front elevation of the complex, while security fencing was kept to the rear. While much softer in visual terms, the reed bed hides a swamp that is as impassable as a fence – meaning it meets the same requirement. While the Centre has been described as a data fortress (Information Age, 2006), the reed bed design solution addresses perimeter access security in a way that is subtle and not visually threatening. In fact, if you weren't told, it would be unlikely that you would realise it was a security feature at all – until you tried to cross it!

While style may be important from a design point of view, it can be equally important from a crime prevention perspective. The visual style of a design can affect users' attitudes and behaviours towards it. Consequently, attractive designs tend to engender care and respect, and are well looked after by users and managers. For example in urban design, anonymous, open and sterile environments often become targets for crime. Users feel insecure and helpless, as they are powerless to control crime and antisocial behaviour. Evidence of environments being uncared for – broken windows, graffiti, rubbish, poorly maintained paintwork and infringements of rules – can lead to a further break-down of law and order and the wider decline of an area. This understanding is reflected in various theories applied to crime and security, which describe how small incidents can precede serious crime problems and precede more general social and economic decline. These include: Malcom Gladwell's (2000) book *The Tipping Point: How Little Things Can Make a Big Difference*; the broken windows theory (Kelling & Coles, 1996; Wilson & Kelling, 1982) and Jane Jacob's *The Death and Life of Great American Cities* (1961).

If more overt security measures are required, then well-considered design can improve even these. For example transparent roller shutters can be used to create a more inviting shop front and do not attract as much graffiti as unsightly metal grilles. German designer Matthias Megyeri created his Sweet Dreams Security fencing as a playful comment on the visual style of 'high-security' products (See Figures 3.1a and 3.1b). Yet despite its visual humour, his fence nevertheless meets the requirements for such barriers, in that it discourages climbing.

Secure and accessible

Designers are under pressure to ensure that products, services and environ-ments are accessible to all types of users. In the architectural design field, public sector clients may be keen to promote social inclusion by connecting differ-ent urban areas, mixing different types of tenure and avoiding the creation of isolated 'gated communities'. However, providing easy access to residential areas can support offenders in committing burglary and vehicle theft. Such

(a)

(b)

Figure 3.1a and 3.1b Sweet Dreams Security railings 'Didoo, R. Bunnit and PeterPin', designed by German designer Matthias Megyeri in 2005.

Source: http://www.iconeye.com/read-previous-issues/icon-028-%7C-october-2005/matthias-megyeri-%7C-icon-028-%7C-october-2005

crimes will impact negatively on residents' quality of life, leading to feelings of fear and even the sense of being trapped in their own homes. The notion of 'access' is not a simple one, and may in fact be a 'crime generator' (Armitage, 2006; Brantingham & Brantingham, 1984). Additional access routes will tend to result in more people moving through an area – some of whom will be potential offenders. Access in relation to a residential neighbourhood may enable offenders to scope potential opportunities, such as a window left open or a home that is routinely unoccupied. In terms of a single dwelling, access may provide potential offenders entry to vulnerable parts of the property, such as a back door that is not overlooked by neighbours.

Designers of the built environment have to find a balance between: (a) the need to facilitate the movement of people and of cars and (b) the impact of movement on crime, antisocial behaviour and feelings of insecurity amongst other users. If footpaths running through residential areas are deemed essential, then these should run alongside roads, and avoid providing access to the rear of properties. Furthermore, for those properties situated close to footpaths, additional security is advisable (ODPM, 2004).

Where the context and associated crime problems are understood by designers, access and security can be combined effectively. Hulme Park, a new public park built in Greater Manchester, UK, was designed to be both accessible and secure for different age groups from the earliest design stage. The park boundary comprises an attractive red brick wall, of about half a metre in height, with a bespoke designed horizontal metal railing system above (see Figure 3.2). Horizontal railings were used for a number of reasons. First, the landscape architect wanted to create a boundary that was visually permeable and so would attract users into the park. Second, the architect wanted to allow children who are wont to climb over railings to be able to do so safely. One concern raised by residents living in housing adjacent to the park boundary was that groups of young people would sit on the railings, 'hanging out' and causing a nuisance. To counter this, the railings were designed with the topmost rail set at an angle that made the fence uncomfortable to sit on. In addition, areas within the park were designed specifically for children and young people, including a play area, youth shelters and sports facilities. To ensure longer life of the boundary design solution, the wall was constructed in discrete sections held together by steel fixings. This allows sections to be replaced relatively easily and cheaply, if the wall is subject to criminal damage or needs repair for some reason (Davey *et al.*, 2002; Town *et al.*, 2003).

Knowledge and resources

Most designers are not experts in security but must learn about offending from the wealth of knowledge already available, and then figure out how to apply such knowledge to their design activities. Information and raw data on crime levels and patterns across the industrialised world are available via the International Crime Victimisation Survey (ICVS) (van Dijk *et al.*, 2007). But

Figure 3.2 Fencing in Hulme Park, Manchester (UK).

Photo © 2002 Design Policy Partnership.

how does this help the designer? Designers need access to qualitative information about offending behaviours, motivations and decision-making that is relevant to their particular design project. Furthermore, such information about offending behaviour needs to be presented in a form that is useful to designers and their process of working. To address crime issues and improve security, designers are primarily concerned with (a) reducing opportunities and (b) influencing offenders to reduce the attractiveness of potential targets or increase the perceived difficulty of committing an offence. Designers can undertake research into offender attitudes, behaviours and motivations using publicly available sources.

Frameworks and models have been developed to help designers understand the causal factors that underpin crime and their impact on offending behaviour in crime situations, as well as generate prevention strategies and solutions. In 2001, while working for the UK Home Office, Paul Ekblom published a framework of causal factors leading up to a crime taking place called 'The Conjunction of Criminal Opportunity'. We adapted and extended Ekblom's framework to consider aspects occurring after a crime incident, developing guidance for design professionals and publishing in 2003 *Crime Lifecycle: Guidance for Generating Design Against Crime Ideas* (Wootton & Davey, 2003). *The Crime Lifecycle* is designed to help designers consider crime issues during the development of design concepts, and take into account factors before and after a crime event.

To effectively address crime issues, crime prevention should be embedded within the design process (Design Council, 2003; 2011). The *Think Thief* publication published by the Design Council (2003) presents a four-stage process to Design Against Crime, and includes the crime lifecycle model to support designers in their efforts to generate innovative, effective solutions.

Of course, real impact on the overall level of crime and insecurity experienced by citizens every day requires not just isolated design projects but a more integrated initiative through which the skills and expertise from across a wide range of design disciplines are brought to bear on the wicked problem of crime prevention. This is the long-term goal of the Design Against Crime initiative.

References

Armitage, R. (2006) 'Predicting and Preventing: Developing a Risk Assessment Mechanism for Residential Housing'. *Crime Prevention and Community Safety: An International Journal*, Vol. 8, No. 3, pp. 137–149.

Brantingham, P.L. and Brantingham, P.J. (1984) 'Burglar Mobility and Preventive Planning'. In R.V. Clarke and T. Hope (eds.) *Coping with Burglary: Research Perspectives on Policy*. Boston: Kluwer-Nijhoff. pp. 77–96.

Davey, C.L., Cooper, R. and Press, M. (2002) *Design Against Crime: Case Study Exemplars*. Salford, UK: Design Policy Partnership.

De Bono, E. (1992) *Serious Creativity: Using the Power of Lateral Thinking to Create New Ideas*. London: Harper Collins.

Design Council. (2003) *Think Thief: A Designer's Guide to Designing Out Crime.* UK Design Council and Design Policy Partnership (based on Design Against Crime: Support material for Design Professionals written by Davey Cooper *et al.*). London: UK Design Council.

Design Council. (2011) *Designing Out Crime: A Designer's Guide.* London: UK Design Council. Original research conducted by the Design Against Crime Solution Centre, University of Salford. Download from: http://www.designcouncil.org.uk/Documents/Documents/OurWork/Crime/designersGuide_digital.pdf

Ekblom, P. (2000) 'Less Crime, by Design'. Presentation at Royal Society of Arts, London, UK, 11th October 2000.

Ekblom, P. (2012) *Design Against Crime: Crime Proofing Everyday Products.* Crime Prevention Studies, Vol. 27, Ronald V. Clarke (Series ed.). Boulder, CO: Lynne Rienner Publishers.

Gladwell, M. (2000) *The Tipping Point: How Little Things Can Make a Big Difference.* London: Abacus.

Information Age. (2006) 'Experian Builds a Data Centre Fortress'. 25 February. Download from: http://www.information-age.com/industry/software/288286/experian-builds-a-data-centre-fortress

Jacobs, J. (February 1993 [1961]) *The Death and Life of Great American Cities.* Modern Library (Hardcover ed.). New York: Random House.

Kelling, G.L. and Coles, C.M. (1996) *Fixing Broken Windows: Restoring Order and Reducing Crime in Our Communities.* New York: Touchstone Books.

ODPM. (2004) *Safer Places: The Planning System and Crime Prevention.* Office of the Deputy Prime Minister and Home Office. Tonbridge, UK: Thomas Telford.

Pease, K. (2001) *Cracking Crime Through Design.* London: UK Design Council. p. 27.

Rouse, W.B. (1991) *Design for Success: A Human-Centred Approach to Designing Successful Products and Systems.* New York: John Wiley and Sons.

Town, S., Davey, C.L. and Wootton, A. (2003) *Design Against Crime: Guidance for the Design of Residential Areas.* Salford, UK: University of Salford. Second edn.

van Dijk, J., van Kesteren, J. and Smit, P. (2007) 'Criminal Victimisation in International Perspective. Key Findings from the 2004–2005 ICVS and EU ICS'. The Hague, Netherlands: WODC.

Wilson, J.Q. and Kelling, G. (1982) 'Broken Windows'. *Atlantic Monthly*, Vol. 249, No. 3, pp. 29–38.

Wootton, A.B. and Davey, C.L. (2003) *Crime Lifecycle: Guidance for Generating Design Against Crime Ideas.* Salford, UK: University of Salford.

Wootton, A.B. and Davey, C.L. (2012) 'Embedding Crime Prevention Within Design'. In P. Ekblom (Guest ed.) *Design Against Crime: Crime Proofing Everyday Products.* Crime Prevention Series, Vol. 27, Ronald V. Clarke (Series ed.). Boulder, CO: Lynne Rienner Publishers.

Websites

Design & Technology Alliance Against Crime. 'The Alliance'. London: UK Design Council. Please refer to: http://www.designcouncil.org.uk/resources/case-study/design-out-crime

Matthias Megyeri, a German graphic artist, established Sweet Dreams Security. Information about his work is available from exhibitions and publications, including:

  • http://www.iconeye.com/read-previous-issues/icon-028-%7C-october-2005/matthias-megyeri-%7C-icon-028-%7C-october-2005

- http://www.detail.de/architektur/themen/matthias-megyeri-acts-of-sweet-dreams-securityR-021058.html
- http://ifitshipitshere.blogspot.de/2008/09/sweet-dreams-security-safety-never

UK Design Council, Designing Out Crime, www.designcouncil.org. 'Projects to Design Out Crime Have Been Archived in the Knowledge and Resources Section'. Download from: http://www.designcouncil.org.uk/knowledge-resources
Examples include:

- The Ultimate Pint Glass. Download from: http://www.designcouncil.org.uk/knowledge-resources/ultimate-pint-glass
- Accident & Emergency Design Challenge Evaluation – AE designed to reduce problem of aggression. Download from: http://www.designcouncil.org.uk/knowledge-resources/ae-design-challenge-impact-evaluation

Part II

Addressing crime prevention within the design process

4 Safety and security

The human perspective

The concepts of security and safety are inextricably interlinked. In English, the concept of 'security' is more often linked with intentional, malevolent harm, whereas the notion of 'safety' is a wider one, also encompassing accidental injury. Unfortunately, the two words are often used interchangeably, making it unclear exactly what is meant. We would suggest that 'safety' is a more experiential term, descriptive of a feeling that can be present or absent in a human user. Security, on the other hand, tends to be used in a more political, technical, instrumental manner – for example in terms such as food security, national security or psychological security. From a human-centred perspective, the experience of crime and insecurity results in feelings of 'unsafety' and anxiety.

The human experience of crime and insecurity reduces enjoyment of products, places and services, potentially deterring future use and impacting negatively on well-being and quality of life. Bill Gates, billionaire founder of Microsoft, highlights security as a critical barrier to the adoption of new technologies by users:

> Security is, I would say, our top priority because for all the exciting things you will be able to do with computers – organising your lives, staying in touch with people, being creative – if we don't solve these security problems, then people will hold back.
>
> (Gates, 2005)

Consequently, designers need to explore and understand user experiences of crime and insecurity that relate to their discipline of design.

This chapter discusses issues relating to the impact of crime on everyday life, drawing on information about victimisation and its consequences from the many studies conducted in this area. Home Office data from 2013 suggests that around 20 per cent of the population of England and Wales were victims of crime during the previous 12 months (CSEW, 2013a; 2013b). However, the issue of insecurity is broader than just the experience of victimisation. It includes contemplating the possibility of becoming a victim, and the anxiety this raises in certain situations, as well as the sense of annoyance at having to take precautions or put up with security procedures. Certain types of crimes will tap into deeply felt emotions, such as fear of vulnerability, humiliation, violation and loss of loved ones, and so will impact on many others besides the immediate victim. Crime and security are social, political and moral issues, about which people have strongly held beliefs and assumptions, and will be open to expressing their opinions. As this chapter highlights, not enough is known about insecurity and its impact on the quality of experience. Recent studies indicate that 'fear of crime' surveys do not effectively differentiate between the feelings, emotions and opinions of respondents. They are also unable to measure the impact of insecurity on well-being or quality of life in a meaningful way. Consequently, further research is needed to understand the wider impact of the experience of victimisation and insecurity on the general population.

The need for safety and security

Safety and security are key issues for users and citizens – and are therefore a topic relevant to the design profession. After food and shelter, the psychologist Abraham Maslow identifies safety as a fundamental human need, from which all other things are possible – love and belonging, esteem and self-actualisation (Maslow, 1943). Freedom from crime is recognised as being important for psychological and physical well-being. Consequently, criteria relating to crime and security are incorporated into measures of well-being and happiness. In 2005, the International Institute of Management proposed a gross national happiness (GNH) metric, which covers factors such as complaints of domestic conflicts, lawsuits and crime rates (IIM, 2006). In the UK, research into well-being conducted by the Office of National Statistics (ONS) includes crime as a factor (ONS, 2016).

Not surprisingly, issues of crime, conflict and stability are considered fundamental to the 'liveability' of a location. Crime is a repelling force, so employees may have to be compensated financially to relocate to a city with high crime or conflict problems, due to the negative impact on well-being and quality of life. Indeed, the *Global Liveability Index* was initially developed to identify locations that require employers to provide more attractive relocation packages to attract and retain staff. The *Liveability Index* produced by *The Economist*'s Intelligence Unit attracts widespread media interest, and the results impact on the perceived attractiveness of cities highlighted in the report (EIU, 2013).

The importance of safety and security for UK citizens

Crime and insecurity are important issues for citizens across Europe, particularly for those living in the UK. In 2008, the market research company Ipsos MORI produced a report on perceptions of crime and justice amongst UK citizens (Duffy *et al.*, 2008). Their research showed that 55 per cent of British people rated crime and violence as the most worrying issue for them. This was of the highest level of concern that Ipsos MORI recorded for any single issue, and was 20 percentage points higher than the second most important issue. When compared to citizens from other European countries, and even the United States, the authors note that crime and violence are more important to British citizens. Crime and insecurity have been prioritised by British governments consistently since 1997, despite the fact that rates of crime have fallen over this time (Duffy *et al.*, 2008). As a result, designers need to explore whether crime and insecurity are issues for users of their designs.

Victims of crime

The incidence of many types of common crimes is falling, but crime continues to directly impact on a significant proportion of UK citizens. Consequently, crime may be an important consideration within a whole range of design projects – especially if the experience impacts on the user's experience and behaviour.

Risk of victimisation in England and Wales

In the 12 months preceding March 2013, there were 8.6 million crimes in England and Wales. We can have confidence in the accuracy of this figure, as it is based on interviews with a representative sample of approximately 50,000 households undertaken for the Crime Survey for England & Wales (CSEW). These prevalence rates were substantially lower than those measured by the CSEW in the mid-1990s. Indeed, the 2013 estimate is the lowest since the survey began in 1981 (CSEW, 2013a, b).

The survey identified that 14 out of every 100 households experienced some type of household crime. In particular, 5 in every 100 households were a victim of vandalism, 5 in every 100 a victim of vehicle crime and 2 in every 100 a victim of burglary – some 468,000 households. In terms of the impact on the individual, 5 in every 100 adults were a victim of crime against the person. In addition, 3 in every 100 adults were a victim of some type of violence.

Prevalence rates for crime vary by crime type, with vandalism and vehicle-related theft both being the most common household crime, at around 5 in

---

Crime Survey for England and Wales

Information about victims of crime is available from the Crime Survey for England and Wales (CSEW) – previously known as the British Crime Survey. Surveys are conducted with a sample of householders across England and Wales to identify experience of common crimes. The survey findings are used to identify the volume of common crimes, risk of victimisations and trends compared to previous years. The results of the CSEW are more reliable than police-recorded data.

Source: CSEW (2013a; 2013b).

every 100 households. Violence, which includes assault and robbery, is the most prevalent crime against the person, with around 3 in every 100 adults becoming a victim.

The likelihood of being a victim of crime decreases with age, with a much higher proportion of adults aged 16 to 24 reporting they had been a victim of personal crime (11.7 per cent) than other age groups. Adults over the age of 75 years are the least likely to be victims of crime (1.3 per cent).

Risk of victimisation

Risk of victimisation is not the same everywhere, but varies from country to country. Parts of Britain suffer from high levels of crime relative to other industrialised countries. The International Crime Victimisation Survey (ICVS) conducted in 2004 and 2005 identified high rates of crime in Ireland, England and Wales, New Zealand and Iceland (van Dijk *et al.*, 2007). Consequently, citizens in these countries are at higher risk of victimisation.

The United States, Canada and Australia were all near to the average rate – which was 16 per cent at that time (van Dijk *et al.*, 2007, p. 42). This may surprise some, as it is commonly assumed the United States suffers from a high level of crime. Relative to other industrialised nations, the United States does experience high levels of violence involving firearms and other weapons, however. The media's role in forming citizens' perceptions of crime and influencing their assessment of risk of victimisation is much discussed. It is suggested that the media's appetite for reporting violent crime may lead people to generalise about all crime, and increase their perception of risk (van Dijk *et al.*, 2007).

Crime rates across Europe

The European Crime and Safety Survey (EU ICS) results published for EU policymakers in 'The Burden of Crime in Europe' reveal the following groupings in terms of crime level:

1   High (significantly higher than the average) – Ireland, United Kingdom, Estonia, the Netherlands, Denmark and Belgium.
2   Medium (not significantly different from the mean) – include Poland, Sweden, Germany and Luxemburg.
3   Low (significantly lower than the average) – Spain, Hungary, Portugal, France, Austria and Greece.

Crime is very much context-dependent, with different types of crime more prevalent in different countries. The risk of being assaulted is particularly high in the United Kingdom, Ireland, the Netherlands, Belgium, Sweden and

Denmark. This is attributed to the high level of alcohol consumption by its citizens (van Dijk *et al.*, 2005).

Within a single country, crime is extremely variable, with the risk of becoming a victim of crime higher in cities than in rural areas. Some capital cities experience particularly high levels of crime – for instance London (UK) and Tallinn (Estonia) (van Dijk *et al.*, 2007, p. 12).

Mobile electronic products used within urban environments, such as mobile phones, put users at increased risk of crime. As mobile phone usage has increased in England and Wales, robberies have also increased. The crime of 'theft from the person' is increasing, with police-recorded crime figures showing a 9 per cent increase in the year ending March 2013 compared with the previous year. With 45 per cent of 'theft-from-the-person' offences concentrated in London, the overall increase in this offence in England and Wales is driven by incidents in this city. There is evidence to suggest that this increase is partly driven by a rise in the number of thefts of mobile phones while being used by the victim (CSEW, 2013a, b).

The impact of crime on victims

The impact on a victim varies significantly depending on factors such as the type of crime, the circumstances of the offence and individual response. Violent crime can result in both physical and psychological harm, and have longer-term negative consequences. Victims of robbery are aware of their property being taken, and are subject to a threat of some sort. In a study by Gale and Coupe (2005), a majority of victims found street robbery to be a 'very frightening experience' that increased fear of crime and resulted in serious psychological distress in many cases. Nine months later the effects had moderated, but robberies were still having a serious and enduring effect on victims' fear, social behaviour and psychological health, particularly for women.

Since burglars tend to avoid breaking into houses that are occupied (Cozens *et al.*, 2001), one might expect that burglary victims are unlikely to be confronted by the burglar. However, two-thirds reported being at home during the burglary when surveyed by Victim Support (2005). Burglary victims are likely to react with shock and anger, and afterwards many feel insecure in their own home. They may feel that their sense of 'home' has been damaged and the sanctity of their personal, private space violated, and may fear further break-ins. The Victim Support survey found that 60 per cent of victims said that they were emotionally affected. Victims of burglary often increase their home security – for instance installing home security systems, better door and window locks and even secure fencing. This is a sensible precaution, and indeed one recommended by the police, due to the known risk of repeat victimisation. Burglars, having familiarised themselves with a house and neighbourhood, frequently return to dwellings and areas in which they have had success. As well as the first burglary providing, in effect, experience useful for future break-ins to the same or similar dwelling type in the area, revisiting a previous burglary scene may offer the opportunity to steal any new items purchased to replace those stolen previously (Clarke *et al.*, 2001; Victim Support, 2005).

While increased security reduces the actual risk of future victimisation, it can also have negative consequences for users, including increased cost and inconvenience. Importantly, such measures may not necessarily make users feel safer. Indeed, if they have the means, victims of burglary may choose to move out of the area. Victims of assault, robbery and threat of violence may avoid places they consider 'risky'. Depending on the nature of the location and method of victimisation, this might include public places, car parks and public transport. As a result, crime not only affects victims, their families and loved ones but is also potentially damaging to communities, and to public and private services.

As shown in Figure 4.1, crime has both tangible and intangible outcomes, which ripple out from the victim, potentially affecting wider society.

Designers need to consider the business implications of crime. Victims of crime may avoid purchasing or using goods and services that potentially put them at risk. For example theft of a bicycle may dissuade future purchase of a new bicycle. Victims of mobile phone theft or robbery may be cautious about upgrading to a new model or using personal electronic devices for financial transactions. Negative experiences impact on user habits, behaviours and choices in ways that can be costly for businesses and wider society. Designers need to be aware of this.

Feelings of insecurity

Being a victim is known to increase worry about crime, but feelings of insecurity are also generated by other factors – some of which are not directly related to actual crime levels. Indeed, feelings of insecurity are on average higher amongst some groups least at risk of crime, and anxiety is focused on crimes that are extremely unlikely to occur.

User groups vulnerable to insecurity

Women and older people are particularly prone to feelings of insecurity. Women's feelings of insecurity focus on concerns about being the victim of sexual violence, particularly rape and sexual assault. Vulnerability to sexual violence may be experienced by victims of more common crimes, such as robbery and burglary, adding to the fear and impact associated with the offence. Female victims may be blamed for taking unnecessary risks, for getting drunk, for wearing provocative clothing and so on. Women are therefore likely to display strong and conflicting feelings about crime and insecurity.

Older people's anxieties arise from a more general feeling of vulnerability, and fear of the consequences of any attack. For instance older people may fear being knocked over and sustaining personal injuries if robbed on the street.

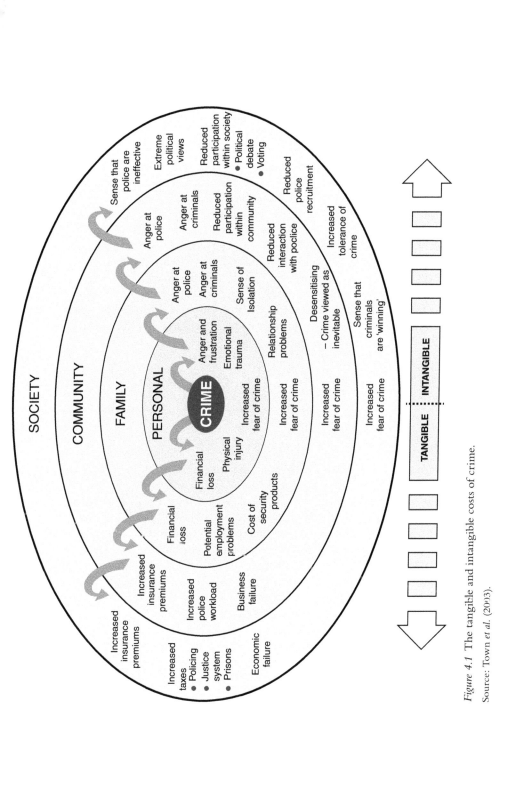

Figure 4.1 The tangible and intangible costs of crime.

Source: Town *et al.* (2003).

Parents are particularly prone to heightened concerns about crime, particularly with regard to harm to their child. This has more to do with the potential consequences rather than actual risk levels.

Child murder: facts versus fears

In England and Wales, the figures for child murder have been largely stable in recent years, at around 50 victims in total each year. In the majority of cases, children who are homicide victims are killed by a parent. Most at risk are children under one year of age. If we look at figures from England and Wales over the last decade, on average around 70 per cent of child homicides where there was a suspect were committed by a parent. Just over 16 per cent were committed by another family member, a friend or an acquaintance, while the remaining 15 per cent were committed by strangers (figures are rounded). The broad trend over the decade is a gradual decrease in the number of child murder victims – and this has occurred despite an increase in pornographic material on the Internet.

Source: The Guardian (2013a).

Urban situations that generate anxieties

Worries about victimisation link to other anxieties, including fear of the dark and feelings of unsafety on the street. Research shows that feelings of insecurity are far from simple. They are generated by a range of environmental factors within public space, including: poor lighting in public areas, graffiti, vandalism, litter on the street, public drunkenness, evidence of drug dealing or taking, and the presence of people considered threatening. For example some people may consider beggars, buskers and young people 'hanging around' in public areas as threatening or anxiety-provoking – especially if such groups are behaving in an uncivil or aggressive manner (Manchin *et al.*, 2005; van Dijk *et al.*, 2005). However, even if such groups are not behaving in a manner that could be described as antisocial, some people will nevertheless find them a source of anxiety. Consequently, designers may need to meet and reconcile the needs of different groups for safety and security.

In fact, many of the factors listed earlier can be unrelated to the actual occurrence of crime, and users may therefore be worrying unnecessarily. Under these circumstances, there is much that can usefully be done from a design perspective to enhance feelings of safety and security. However, it is important to note the design features should not increase feelings of safety if this encourages behaviour that increases risk of victimisation. For example some parks in

high-crime areas are unlit after dark to discourage their use. Adding lighting would encourage late-night use – for example as a shortcut home – and
thereby increase users' risk of becoming victims of robbery and assault.

Feelings of insecurity across Europe

Feelings of insecurity are issues in some countries with medium or low levels of actual crime, such as Greece, Portugal, Luxembourg, Spain and Italy.
Research suggests that this is due to environmental factors, such as citizens
being aware of drug dealing on the streets and seeing syringes left in parks
(Manchin *et al.*, 2005; van Dijk *et al.*, 2005).

Sometimes citizens or users feel safe despite potential dangers. Danish citizens, for instance, report feeling safe despite relatively high levels of crime
compared to other European countries (Manchin *et al.*, 2005; van Dijk *et al.*,
2005).

Despite the decrease in crime rates across Europe, feelings of insecurity have
not necessarily declined to the same degree. Feelings of unsafety on the street
have not declined significantly, despite reductions in violent crime. However,
somewhat fewer residents are concerned that their houses will be burgled –
which is in line with actual decreases in burglary rates in many countries
(Manchin *et al.*, 2005; van Dijk *et al.*, 2005).

Worry about service security and new technologies

Some worries focus less on personal safety and more on the security of services
used for activities such as purchasing goods, banking and communication.
Vulnerability to crime when using services can generate unease, reduce satisfaction and result in precautionary and often inconvenient security measures
having to be taken. New technologies and finances are a source of stress for
many people, and particularly for older age groups. The potential impact of
Internet security issues on quality of life should perhaps not be underestimated,
especially as users are subjected relatively frequently to efforts to defraud them.
Any new Internet interaction raises questions about the reliability of the source,
the risks of sharing personal information and the security of financial transactions. Worries about the security of Internet services deter users in England
and Wales from purchasing goods online or using online banking services.

Cybercrime

The majority of people in England and Wales use the Internet, especially
within the young age groups. Over half of users take action to protect
their personal details online. Adult users of the Internet worry about
security, especially for certain uses. Forty-four per cent of adults who
had used the Internet for buying goods or services online said they were

worried about the security of personal details. Twenty-six per cent of adults gave this reason for not buying goods and services online. Thirty-seven per cent who used the Internet for banking or managing finances worried, and concern about personal details being insecure online was given as a reason by 34 per cent of adults for not using the Internet for online banking or managing finances.

Source: Home Office (2012).

People worry that societal changes and technological developments will open up possibilities for new forms of crime, and this issue is considered in the last chapter.

Emerging crimes: fact versus fiction

In 2012, the Home Office published a special bulletin titled 'Hate Crime, Cyber Security and the Experience of Crime Among Children'. The numbers come from the 2010/11 Crime Survey, and are not therefore up to date, but they do ask Internet users over the age of 16 about their 'negative experiences' online. Just 2 per cent of all Internet users said they had experienced abusive/threatening behaviour in the past year. However, that number was significantly higher for young people: 6 per cent of women aged 16–24 and 5 per cent of men aged 16–24. A higher proportion said they had seen upsetting images, but these were not necessarily targeted at the user.

Source: The Guardian (2013b) and Home Office (2012).

Perceptions of crime and security

People have strongly held views about crime, the extent to which it's a problem, how it should be dealt with and so on. Some of these beliefs contrast significantly with the evidence.

Misperceptions about crime levels

It would appear that the UK public is misinformed about crime. The majority of people do not believe that crime is falling, despite evidence of reductions in the number of incidents. An Ipsos MORI poll in 2008 reported that only one in five UK citizens is willing to accept that crime is falling. Misperceptions about crime arise from the media's focus on negative stories about crime. In an Ipsos MORI poll conducted in 2007, members of the public were asked what made them think there is more crime than two years ago. Fifty-seven per cent said what they saw on TV, and 48 per cent said what they read in the newspaper. Public opinion may also be influenced by particular high-profile problems or cases, such as injury from firearms – which had increased leading up to 2008 (Duffy *et al.*, 2008).

The 2014 report by the National Audit Office (NAO) states that police crime figures are unreliable due to biases in reporting, and this has been widely reported in the media (Travis, 2014). However, the evidence of falling rates of crime comes primarily from victimisation surveys. Unfortunately, evidence of bias in police records may lead citizens to distrust all sources of data on crime levels.

Views on criminal justice

Designers and other stakeholders need to be aware of the complexity and contradictory nature of public attitudes about crime and justice. It is not just that different people hold different views, but that the same person can also be inconsistent in his or her attitudes. An Ipsos MORI report shows that people want tougher sentences, but are not convinced that prison works. When asked to 'sentence' cases themselves, they are not especially punitive. Their preference would be for more preventative measures (Duffy *et al.*, 2008).

People may express doubts about the effectiveness of better security, but use security devices to protect valuables – clearly believing that devices such as locks and alarms help to prevent crime.

Fear of crime, insecurity and quality of life

Fear of crime is an enduring topic that has been considered since the 1960s in the United States and 1970s in the UK (Farrall, 2007). Indeed, fear of crime is one of the few more subjective issues to be measured since 1982 by the British Crime Survey (now called the Crime Survey in England and Wales). However, some people who report being 'very worried about crime' can't actually remember incidents of worry over the last year. This suggests that worries do not actually impact on everyday experience or quality of life. This raises thorny questions about how to measure feelings of insecurity, and whether current methods have perhaps misrepresented or indeed exaggerated the 'problem'.

Rethinking fear of crime measures

Professor Stephen Farrall (2007) found that what previously had been identified as 'fear of crime' can usefully be divided into two phenomena:

1   *Everyday worry about crime*, which is relatively rare and typically affects those who live in high-crime areas with direct and indirect experience of crime

2   *Anxiety about crime*, which is more widespread and typically affects those who lead more protected lives.

The concept of 'fear of crime' is complicated by the fact that people do not separate out crime from other interrelated issues, such as social cohesion, collective efficacy, social change and tension. People do not have an irrational fear of crime *per se*, but rather within worries or anxieties purportedly about crime lie concerns about social breakdown, stability and the violation of social rules. The research conducted by Farrall and his colleagues shows that both everyday worries and more general anxieties about crime are strongly related to anxieties about neighbourhood order, cohesion, collective efficacy and trust. Such local anxieties are also associated with broader and more diffuse societal concerns about moral order, agreed social norms and the social bonds that connect people (Farrall, 2007; Farrall *et al.*, 2007a; 2007b; Gray *et al.*, 2011).

Fear of crime: a misleading term

There is a lot written about 'fear of crime' and the term confusingly is used to embrace a whole range of feelings, including beliefs about social issues and more general fears of the dark, crowded public places and so on. We therefore prefer to talk about anxieties and worries about crime, and to reserve the term fear of crime for situations where an individual perceives a risk of becoming a victim of crime and experiences fear – that is being scared for his or her own personal safety or well-being.

Source: Davey and Wootton (2014).

The next chapters will discuss how to address crime, antisocial behaviour and related social issues within the design process.

References

Clarke, R., Perkins, E. and Smith Jr., D. (2001) 'Explaining Repeat Residential Burglaries: An Analysis of Property Stolen'. In G. Farrell and K. Pease (eds.) *Repeat Victimization*. Crime Prevention Studies, Vol. 12. Monsey, NY: Criminal Justice Press. Download from: http://www.popcenter.org/library/crimeprevention/volume_12/07-ClarkePerkins.pdf
Cozens, P., Hillier, D. and Prescott, G. (2001) 'Crime and the Design of Residential Property – Exploring the Perceptions of Planning Professionals, Burglars and Other Users: Part 2'. *Property Management*, Vol. 19, No. 4, pp. 222–248.
CSEW. (2013a) 'Crime Survey in England and Wales'. Year ending March 2013. London: Office for National Statistics, Statistical Bulletin. Download full report from: http://www.ons.gov.uk/ons/dcp171778_318761.pdf

CSEW. (2013b) 'The Likelihood of Becoming a Victim of Crime'. Part of Crime Statistics, period ending March 2013 Release. London: Office of National Statistics. Released: 18 July. Download from: http://webarchive.nationalarchives.gov.uk/20160105160709/ http://www.ons.gov.uk/ons/rel/crime-stats/crime-statistics/period-ending-march-2013/sty-a-victim-of-crime.html

Davey, C.L. and Wootton, A.B. (2014) 'Crime and the Urban Environment. The Implications for Wellbeing'. In R. Cooper, E. Burton and C.L. Cooper (eds.) *Wellbeing and the Environment. Wellbeing: A Complete Reference Guide*, Vol. II. Chichester: John Wiley & Sons.

Duffy, B., Wake, R., Burrows, T. and Bremner, P. (2008) 'Closing the Gap. Crime and Public Perceptions'. London: Ipsos MORI Social Research Institute. Download from: http://www.ipsos.com/public-affairs/sites/www.ipsos.com.public-affairs/files/documents/closing_the_gaps.pdf

EIU. (2013) 'A Summary of the Liveability Ranking and Overview'. *The Economist Intelligence Unit*, August 2013. Download from: http://www.eiu.com/Handlers/Whitepaper Handler.ashx?fi=WEB_Liveability_rankings_Promotional_August_2013.pdf&mode=wp&campaignid=Liveability2013

Farrall, S. (2007) 'Experience and Expression in the Fear of Crime: Full Research Report ESRC End of Award Report'. RES-000–23–1108. Swindon: ESRC. Download from: http://www.esrc.ac.uk/my-esrc/grants/res-000-23-1108/outputs/Read/f7eb73bb-e568-427c-a73f-fd9a4b18370b

Farrall, S., Gray, E. and Jackson, J. (2007a) 'Theorising the Fear of Crime: The Cultural and Social Significance of Insecurities About Crime'. Experience and Expression in the Fear of Crime Working Paper No. 5, ESRC Grant RES-000–23–1108. Download from: http://papers.ssrn.com/sol3/papers.cfm?abstract_id=1012393

Farrall, S., Jackson, J. and Gray, E. (2007b) 'Experience and Expression in the Fear of Crime'. Working Paper, Number 1. ESRC Grant RES-000–23–1108.

Gale, J.-A. and Coupe, T. (2005) 'The Behavioural, Emotional and Psychological Effects of Street Robbery on Victims'. *International Review of Victimology*, January, Vol. 12, No. 1, pp. 1–22.

Gates, B. (2005) 'One-on-One with Bill'. Peter Jennings Interviews Bill Gates, ABC News. Redmond, WA, 16 February 2005. Download from: http://abcnews.go.com/WNT/CEO Profiles/story?id=506354&page=1

Gray, E., Jackson, J. and Farrall, S. (2011) 'Feelings and Functions in the Fear of Crime: Applying a New Approach to Victimisation Insecurity'. *British Journal of Criminology*, Vol. 51, No. 1, pp. 75–94. Download from: http://bjc.oxfordjournals.org/content/51/1/75

The Guardian. (2013a) 'April Jones Murder: The Broader Context'. *Guardian DataBlog*. James Ball and Mona Chalabi, Friday 31 May. Download from: http://www.theguardian.com/news/datablog/2013/may/31/april-jones-child-murder-online-abuse

The Guardian. (2013b) 'How Prevalent Is Online Abuse?'. *The Guardian*. Reality Check. Posted by Mona Chalabi, Monday 29 July. Download from: http://www.theguardian.com/politics/reality-check/2013/jul/29/online-abuse-twitter-social-media

Home Office. (2012) 'Hate Crime, Cyber Security and the Experience of Crime Among Children'. Findings from the 2010/11 British Crime Survey. Supplementary Volume 3 to Crime in England and Wales 2010/11. London: Statistical Bulletin, Home Office. Download from: https://www.gov.uk/government/uploads/system/uploads/attachment_data/file/116465/hosb0612snr.pdf

IIM. (2005) Happiness Economics Gross National Happiness & Wellness Index. Working Paper, 4 January 2005. Las Vegas: Institute of International Management. Download from:

https://www.iim-edu.org/thinktank/publications/economics-journal/gnh-index-gnw-index/index.htm

Manchin, Robert, van Dijk, Jan, Kury, Helmut and Schaber, Gaston. (2005) 'The EU ICS 2005: Highlights and Policy Implications'. Download from: http://www.europeansafety observatory.eu/doc/EUICS%20policy%20implications.pdf

Maslow, A.H. (1943) 'A Theory of Human Motivation'. *Psychological Review*, Vol. 50, No. 4, pp. 370–396.

ONS. (2016) 'Measures of National Wellbeing. Measuring What Matters. Understanding the Nation's Well-being'. Issued March 2016. London: Office of National Statistics. Downloaded from: http://www.neighbourhood.statistics.gov.uk/HTMLDocs/dvc146/wrapper.html (accessed 22.09.2016).

Town, S., Davey, C.L. and Wootton, A. (2003) Design Against Crime: Guidance for the Design of Residential Areas. Second edn. Salford, UK: University of Salford.

Travis, A. (2014) 'Police Crime Figures Lose Official Status over Claims of Fiddling'. *The Guardian*, Wednesday 15 January. Download from: http://www.theguardian.com/uk-news/2014/jan/15/police-crime-figures-status-claims-fiddling

van Dijk, Jan, Manchin, Robert, van Kesteren, John, Nevala, Sami and Hideg, Gergely. (2005) 'The Burden of Crime in the EU. Research Report: A Comparative Analysis of the European Crime and Safety Survey (EU ICS) 2005'. Download from: http://vorige.nrc.nl/redactie/binnenland/Misdaad.pdf (accessed 07.02. 2014).

van Dijk, J.J.M., van Kesteren, J.N. and Smit, P. (2007) 'Criminal Victimisation in International Perspective. Key findings from the 2004–2005 ICVS and EU ICS'. The Hague: Boom Legal. Download from: http://www.unicri.it/services/library_documentation/publications/icvs/publications/ICVS2004_05report.pdf

Victim Support. (2005) 'Investigating the Practical Support Needs of Burglary Victims'. December. London: Victim Support National Office. Download from: http://www.victimsupport.org.uk/~/media/Files/Publications/ResearchReports/investigating-practical-needs.ashx

Website

CSEW. (2013) 'Statistical Bulletin: Crime in England and Wales, Year Ending March 2013'. Crime Survey England and Wales. Download from: http://www.ons.gov.uk/ons/rel/crime-stats/crime-statistics/period-ending-march-2013/stb-crime-period-ending-march-2013.html#tab-Theft-offences-Other-theft-of-property

5 Integrating crime prevention within design development

For the police and the security industry, security and crime prevention are the main priorities. In contrast, designers of everyday products and places must consider a wide range of sometimes conflicting project requirements and constraints. Prevention of crime, antisocial behaviour or feelings of insecurity must be achieved without compromising other desirable objectives. For prevention to be incorporated effectively into a design solution, issues of crime and insecurity need to be considered during the early concept stage of the design process. This effective integration of crime prevention within design is key, as the Design Council identifies: 'Reducing the vulnerability to crime of a product, service or environment is not something that can be done by halves. Bolt-ons don't work. The more integrated the process, the more seamless the outcome will be' (Design Council, 2003, p. 19).

This chapter outlines how vulnerability to crime and insecurity can be incorporated into the design development process. The focus is on the early stages of the design process, involving: the initial identification of crime risks; the inclusion of prevention objectives within the briefing activities; and the exploration of crime and security issues through more detailed research. A detailed account of how to test and validate the design concepts and solutions in terms of crime prevention is provided in Chapter 6.

Considering crime issues from the outset

Depending on the type of project, the process of developing a design can take weeks or months to complete. In the case of the urban environment, it generally takes years to realise a design solution. Overt security devices that are bulky, inconvenient and not in keeping with the overall design aesthetic tend to be employed in situations where crime issues have not been considered during the early stages of the design development. Bolting on security devices to the design is the only practical option when such issues are considered only at a late stage. Not only has the detailed design work been completed by then, but also the design solution has been approved by the client. Any attempt to integrate crime prevention into the proposed design is likely to require a complete reworking of the design solution, and is therefore time-consuming and costly.

When crime issues are considered during the early stages of urban develop-ment, security can be embodied within the design itself – within its function, use, repair, maintenance and so on. For instance the building envelope can be employed to reduce illegitimate entry to the building and a well-designed reception to both control access to the building and improve the quality of the experience for visitors and staff. Any overt security measures deemed neces-sary can be fully integrated into the design. For instance CCTV can be located appropriately to ensure clear images are obtained and communicated to staff responsible for customer service, building management or security. Unfortu-nately, it is not uncommon for potential crime issues to be raised late in the design process. Within many regions of the UK, architects are made aware of crime risks only when submitting a development design for planning approval (Wootton *et al.*, 2009). At this stage, it is often too late to consider improving security through, for example, changes to the design layout. As a result, it is more likely that 'target hardening' features, such as fences and CCTV, will be bolted on to the overall design solution.

Responsibility for highlighting safety and security

There may be some debate about who precisely is responsible for raising safety and security as a design concern. This issue is complicated by the fact that a design project is usually initiated by a client or employer, and a design team recruited or employed to undertake the design work. The initiation stage of a design development project will usually involve an opportunity or problem being identified, business and project objectives being set and a design team being recruited or established to undertake the design work and achieve said objectives. When setting up a development project, research will generally

---

Client awareness of crime issues

The client – and indeed other key stakeholder groups – may not be aware of crime issues relating to their product, system or project area. In our experience, urban planners are sometimes unaware of the exact nature of crime problems associated with the design and use of specific urban areas. This may be because they do not live in the area or visit the area late in the evening, but may also be due to inaccurate perceptions of the causes and extent of problems at different times of the day. Empirical evidence, such as video footage, can be used to provide planners with a more accurate picture of the problems facing areas of their city and town centres – for instance on Friday and Saturday nights. Undesirable behaviours can be identified, and design changes proposed to mitigate these. These include physical alterations, as well as changes to the design of services and urban management processes.

be conducted to determine its viability and scope. So ideally, this project set-up effort should include research to identify whether the proposed project or design outcome is likely to be affected by crime or security issues. This work might take the form of desk research. For example information about previous designs being the target of crime or misuse may be readily available from customer feedback records, maintenance reports and so on. This information would be included as material to support the design brief.

However, not all clients or employers will be aware of the potential for crime issues to impact on a design, in which case, the designers should briefly explore any potential risks and raise the results with their client or employer when responding to the brief.

Identifying potential safety and security issues

Safety and security issues should be explored in relation to all design projects, preferably from the outset – even if only to discount them as issues. Clearly, not every designed product, service or environment risks being vulnerable to crime. It depends on the nature of the design outcome and its context of use. For example in the domestic context, coat hangers would not normally be associated with crime or security issues. However, in the retail sector, the design of coat hangers and the hanging systems on which they are used do have crime implications. The standard design of coat hangers fails to take into account the modus operandi (MO) of professional shoplifters, who will attempt to quickly slide multiple garments off a rail into a bag unseen.

In relation to design, crime risk can be the result of several factors. These can be organised into four broad categories:

1   *The design itself is targeted by criminals* – This is when the design type falls into a high-risk category. For example checks should be undertaken to see whether the design will be CRAVED and a so-called hot product (Clarke, 1999). However, as we pointed out, a whole range of items may be vulnerable to crime within certain environments, including hotel towels and bathrobes and office supplies in the workplace.
2   *The design provides the opportunity for misuse* – A small proportion of users may themselves be offenders or misusers, seeking to use products and services without payment or illegally copying products. DVDs, CDs, downloads, apps and software being used, copied or distributed without paying is a common issue, for instance.
3   *The target users are vulnerable to crime or feelings of insecurity* – For some groups of users, crime is a major concern, despite a lower risk relative to young men – for example women and older people, or parents who worry about the security of their children. In reality, young men are at highest risk of crime – both as victims and perpetrators. Other groups at risk of becoming victims of crime are students, people on low incomes and tourists (CSEW, 2013a; 2013b). Some groups of users are prone to act carelessly, or

are reluctant to take preventative measures. This may be due to a fatalistic belief that any action on their part would not make any difference, or because it would not be considered 'cool' to do so.

Selwyn (2009) surveyed 1,215 UK higher education undergraduate students to examine rationalisations for falling victim to crime while at university. The survey showed just under a third were a victim of crime during the previous three months, with victimisation an often accepted element of student life. Selwyn suggests that to improve their security situation requires fundamentally changing students' expectations and understandings of the student lifestyle. He identified 'prevailing student cultures' as the basis for their often passive responses to being victims of crime.

4   *The design's context of use provides opportunity for victimisation* – The way in which a designed product or system is used, or the context within which it is used, may generate crime issues. How and where a design is kept, transported and used can affect the user's risk of victimisation. The risk is potentially higher for products whose use: is easily visible by offenders (e.g. used in the public realm); involves being carried on the person; or means they are likely to be left unattended (e.g. left in a parked car).

Users of designs vulnerable to crime tend to be at higher risk in towns and cities, compared with less populated environments. Indeed, risk of burglary, assault and criminal damage is generally higher in urban areas. Within cities, certain locations will attract more criminal activity and antisocial behaviour. For example crime is often concentrated around transport hubs, such as train stations and underground stations, but also facilities such as bus stops. Such locations are attractive to thieves due to their concentrations of people, many of whom will be carrying valuables and so be potential targets. High concentrations of people can also generate conflict situations, especially if many are under the influence of alcohol or drugs. This is the problem faced by the police on Friday and Saturday nights in many UK towns and cities. Locations used by young people may be particularly susceptible to crime and antisocial behaviour, including routes to school, parks, public spaces and places where young people 'hang out'. As mentioned previously, young people are at higher risk of being victims of crime than other age groups.

Unused or unsupervised areas can be vulnerable to certain types of crime. Retail areas often become vulnerable to property and criminal damage in the evening when closed to shoppers, and commercial premises may be targeted when closed over the weekend.

In practice, each of the four factors outlined earlier will interact to produce or prevent a problem. For instance a previously safe location may become dangerous because it contains a service attractive to criminals, such as a poorly located cashpoint.

Sources of information

- *Hot products*

  Information on the topic of hot products is available from Ronald V. Clarke (1999). Hot Products. Police Research Series. Paper 112. London: Home Office. Accessible at: www.popcenter.org

- *Mobile phone theft*

  Information on the topic of mobile phone theft is available from Harrington, V. and Mayhew, P. (2001) 'Mobile Phone Theft. Home Office Research Study'. Home Office Development and Practice Report No. 17. London: Home Office.

- *Victimisation in England and Wales*

  Information on crime risk can be obtained from the Crime Survey for England and Wales, available from the UK Home Office.
  CSEW (2013a) The Likelihood of Becoming a Victim of Crime. Part of Crime Statistics, period ending March 2013 Release, Office for National Statistics; London, UK. Released: 18 July, see: http://www.ons.gov.uk/ons/rel/crime-stats/crime-statistics/period-ending-march-2013/sty-a-victim-of-crime.html
  CSEW (2013b) Crime in England and Wales, Year Ending March 2013. Office for National Statistics, Statistical Bulletin, London, UK. Download full report from: http://www.ons.gov.uk/ons/dcp171778_318761.pdf

- *Victimisation worldwide*

  Information on the topic of victimisation worldwide is available from van Dijk, J., van Kesteren, J. and Smit, P. (2007) Criminal Victimisation in International Perspective. Key findings from the 2004–2005 ICVS and EU ICS. The Hague, Netherlands: WODC. Available to download from: http://www.unicri.it/services/library_documentation/publications/icvs/publications/ICVS2004_05report.pdf

The design input

For those readers from other professions and disciplines, it is worth briefly discussing how designers operate and apply their skills. As we said, a project is usually set up by the client or the employer and a design team recruited or employed at a point during the development process, preferably early on so that they can contribute at the project set-up phase.

From the designers' perspective, the early stages of design development involve the creative exploration of ideas and the conception and development of a concept that meets needs and requirements. According to the Design Council, this requires designers to engage in two different modes of thinking (www.designcouncil.org):

- *Divergent thinking* – where ideas and concepts are generated, explored and expanded
- *Convergent thinking* – where ideas and concepts are narrowed down, developed in more detail and refined

Creative processes

The divergent or creative side of design is well recognised. Indeed, the ability to think creatively around problems and develop innovative solutions that meet different stakeholder needs is arguably unique to design. This ability differentiates the design profession from groups responsible for developing solutions to crime problems, such as police and crime prevention experts. It should also be recognised that creative ideas are not a mysterious outcome of abstract 'creative thoughts'. Rather creativity results from concrete efforts to understand human emotions, attitudes, perceptions and behaviours, and the context within which they take place. Innovative ideas are inspired by observation, exploration and research, becoming workable and hopefully inspirational as a result of more painstaking exploration and development.

When working on a project, crime issues ideally need to be considered from the outset, and relevant information provided where available, including reports of crime risk, modus operandi of offenders and good practice principles. In addition, the designers should be supported in their efforts to understand emotions, feelings and behaviours related to crime and insecurity issues.

Evaluative processes

It is not enough to generate lots of creative or even innovative ideas. Ideas must be evaluated in terms of their potential and the best ones selected for further development. Many creative ideas will be generated during this creative process. Some of the ideas will be developed into design concepts, and perhaps several considered for further development. One idea – possibly more – will probably be developed into the detailed design, and may perhaps be taken all the way through to manufacture and launch onto the market. However, it may be that the idea does not progress to manufacture, or indeed to detailed design. Many ideas will prove unsuitable for some reason, including cost and being unattractive to users and unsuitable for the current market. How far an idea progresses also depends on a whole range of factors, not necessarily related to the quality of the idea, including support from senior management and key members of staff, fit with business strategy, company workload and so on.

The evaluative parts of the process involve rigorous research, concept development and feasibility testing. These activities help ensure that the final design will be fit for the purpose, and will meet the needs and requirements of the different stakeholders – especially users. Designers need to dedicate time and resources to activities to improve the chances of success of the design.

Reducing vulnerability to crime will be just one of a range of desirable objectives to be considered. Furthermore, any design solution will be subject to rigorous testing before being fully developed into the final design, including those related to crime prevention.

Commercial factors

The costs and benefits of incorporating crime prevention into the design will be a key consideration for the client, and the design team will take this into account, of course. The further the idea progresses, the greater the level of investment required. Greater investment is likely to be approved by the client or senior management only if a strong business case can be built. Business success is not just about profit, but potentially relates to a range of factors, including client satisfaction and exploitation of an opportunity to develop a new component or product range.

New product development – a formal approach

Research undertaken since the 1960s on success factors in new product development (NPD) suggests that success is best achieved via the adoption of a systematic, well-executed design process (Cooper & Kleinschmidt, 1987; 1995; Kleinschmidt, 1989). While most designers follow some kind of 'design process', the form that this takes and the extent to which it is 'formalised' will vary depending upon the design discipline, the industry context, the complexity of the project and individual/team preferences.

Designers will need to incorporate crime prevention into the design process. Models and more detailed procedures have been developed to conceptualise the design process, as well as support the development process. The Design Council highlights alternating divergent and convergent thinking, resulting in the double diamond form, and identifies four distinct phases of the design development process – discover, define, develop and deliver.

Diamonds are forever

Drawing on the NPD research literature and the DAC Evaluation Framework (Wootton & Davey, 2005), the double diamond has been extended to reflect a more holistic, 'cradle-to-grave' design lifecycle perspective. To this end, a third diamond has been introduced, formed by the two phases of deploy and digest. This third diamond deals with the period when the designed product, service or environment is actually being used 'in the wild' (see Figure 5.1).

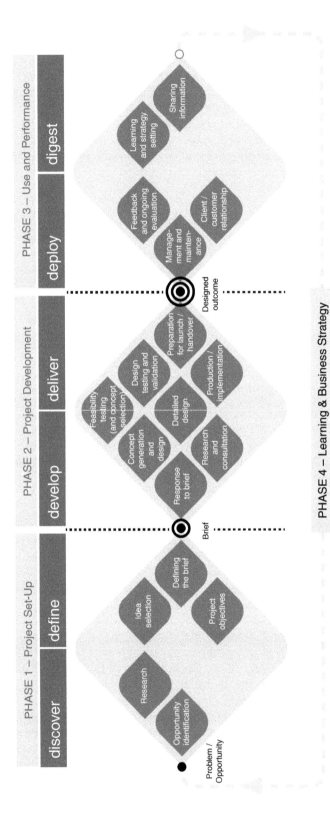

Figure 5.1 The triple diamond model (Wootton & Davey, 2011).

For a designed product, this third diamond is when the distribution and sales of a designed outcome are growing, and when use is spreading. This period covers the following:

- Efforts undertaken to understand how the designed outcome is performing (e.g. sales tracking, user acceptance/satisfaction, technical performance)
- Learning arising from this (e.g. relating to any performance shortfall, unexpected user behaviour, or potential improvements)
- The sharing of this knowledge within the business and with relevant external partners/stakeholders (e.g. the external design consultancy involved in the original development).

As such, this third diamond is concerned with processes, procedures and activities relating to the following:

- Management and maintenance
- Feedback and ongoing evaluation
- Client and customer relationships
- Learning and strategy setting
- Sharing of information.

In this third diamond, insight may be gained regarding a problem or opportunity, which may lead to a new development cycle – and so back to the first diamond. This possibility is indicated in the triple diamond model by the dotted line. Such new developments may be incremental (building on and improving a current design), new to the business or even new to the world.

Of course, not all design projects will make it to the third diamond. While some opportunities will move from a concept to become a design that is realised, built and launched, others will be abandoned at some stage before launch – most often because the business case is not made.

Phases of development

Four phases of development can be identified in the triple diamond model. These relate to the three activity diamonds and the feedback loop, as follows:

> *Phase 1: Project set-up* – Objectives are established and a team established to complete the project within a specific timescale and budget. The project objectives and requirements may be summarised in a briefing document, which forms the start of the next phase. If no internal designers or design managers are involved in these activities, then the first design input will come in Phase 2.
>
> *Phase 2: Project development* – This is when designers generally discuss the brief with the client and their response to it. The bulk of the detailed research and consultation to explore and understand requirements and constraints takes place in Phase 2. The importance of the different

stakeholders must be identified to enable trade-offs to be made, where necessary. The findings are used to develop a design specification, and to support the design team when it comes to generating and testing design concepts – that is ideas for a design. Concept generation and feasibility test activities are often performed iteratively. The design concept selected through feasibility testing is taken through to the detailed design phase. The designer's goal is to create a finished design that meets all the requirements and constraints identified in the research and consultation phase. The detailed design and testing and validation activities are performed iteratively. The design solution is refined and amended until it completes testing and validation satisfactorily, and final production/ implementation activities can begin. The production/implementation activities transform the plans, drawings and written documents that design the design solution into reality. Phase 2 concludes with the design solution being launched or handed over to the owner.

Phase 3: Use and performance – The design is used, managed and maintained, and its performance monitored and evaluated to enable learning to occur. During this phase, activities may be undertaken to help maintain and build the relationship with an external client.

Phase 4: Learning and business strategy – Knowledge is used to improve performance and identify emerging opportunities.

Key project activities

Safety and security issues should be addressed within key project activities, within the design process, as outlined ahead.

In Phase 1 – project set-up

Project objectives and briefing

Where relevant, safety and security should be covered within the list of SMART objectives. SMART is an acronym that stands for: **S**pecific; **M**easurable; **A**chievable; **R**ealistic; **T**ime-based. In our experience, companies sometimes assume that crime issues will be covered under broader objectives related to sustainability or social cohesion. Occasionally, companies appear unwilling to include crime issues in project objectives and/or briefing documents – perhaps due to concerns about negative publicity. We found that crime issues tend to be overlooked if not specifically included with the project objectives (Davey *et al.*, 2009).

The brief – considering crime issues

The design brief should include the following:

- *Crime prevention objectives* – These should be SMART (i.e. Specific; Measurable; Achievable; Realistic; and Time-based – for further

information, see http://www.natpact.info/uploads/Ten%20Steps%20
to%20SMART%20objectives.pdf).

- *Background information about the problem* – This should summarise the nature and scale of the actual security problem, and
  highlight any potential security problems that might occur in the
  future. Details about the cost of the problem would also be useful.
- *Causal factors* – This should contain details of offender modus
  operandi (MO) and user behaviour, especially where this contributes to crime risk. Information about the vulnerability of designs,
  location of crimes and the contribution of environmental factors
  should also be provided, if possible.
- *Potential solution directions* – This should contain information
  about solutions on the market. In some cases, potential strategies for
  addressing the problem might also be presented.
- *Trade-offs and priorities* – This might indicate potential trade-offs
  to consider, highlighting any priorities for the client (e.g. the design
  should be able to prevent crime, but also be easy to use, attractive to
  users, easy to manufacture).
- *Sources of information* – This might include websites, details of con-
  tacts (e.g. users, police, crime prevention experts), articles, written user
  scenarios, images, video (e.g. from TV documentaries, CCTV footage), reports and presentations on offender and/or user behaviour.
- *Selection criteria* – The experience of addressing crime or related
  social issues might be included.

Source: Adapted by Davey and Wootton (2010) from the Designing Out Crime case
studies initiated by the Design Council.

The response to the brief provided by the design team should cover crime
and insecurity issues relevant to users and other stakeholders. The level of
detail provided will depend on the relevance of the issues and the interest of
the client in making a product or service more secure. Ideally, the response to
the brief should demonstrate that the design team:

1   Is aware of the potential relevance of crime and security issues by:

- Providing information about crime and insecurity. This should cover
  the nature and scale of the actual security problem, any potential
  security problems that might occur in the future and actual or potential cost of crime.
- Highlighting potential risks of crime due to the nature of the product
  (e.g. CRAVED) and/or context of use (e.g. carried, used in high-
  crime areas).

2   Intends to conduct further research to understand the problem and generate solutions by:

- Consulting sources of information on offender modus operandi, user behaviour, vulnerability of designs, location of crimes and the contribution of environmental factors. Sources of information include police officers and websites, such as http://www.popcenter.org.

3   Intends to identify potential solutions to problems by:

- Investigating potential solutions/approaches to crime prevention that are already on the market.
- Generating solutions to crime problems using, for example, the crime lifecycle model.

4   Is aware of the need to consider priorities and trade-offs by:

- Highlighting how research and consultation will identify user needs, stakeholder priorities and potential trade-offs.

5   Is able to bring appropriate knowledge, skills and experience to the project by:

- Having gained experience in addressing crime or related social issues.
- Having knowledge of strategic issues such as CSR.
- Consulting with experts and/or offenders.

In Phase 2 – project development

Research and consultation

Within the design process, research and consultation activities are undertaken to better understand the project requirements and constraints. In some industries this activity is known as 'requirements capture' (Wootton *et al.*, 1998). The impact on project success of gaining a good understanding of issues and problems at an early stage is well recognised. Indeed, in manufacturing projects, the time and effort spent at the 'front end' of the development process have proven to be a key factor in differentiating successes from failures. Typical activities include desk-based research, interviews with stakeholders, site visits and observation of user behaviour. Information about vulnerability to crime, offender behaviours and modi operandi (MOs) and design principles is available from various sources (see the following box).

Consultation about security and safety may be conducted with: clients/customers, users (especially vulnerable groups), potential misusers, management and maintenance personnel, crime experts (e.g. local police) and design-led crime prevention experts (e.g. police architectural liaison officers – ALOs).

Sources of information on crime and security

- *Problem-oriented policing (US)* – There are around 60 guides covering issues such as financial crimes, robbery of commercial premises, commercial burglary, shoplifting, markets in stolen products, domestic burglary, theft from cars, bicycle theft, vandalism, graffiti, disorderly behaviour and bullying. Each guide provides information about the crime/problem, the victims, the offenders (including MO) and locations and times of crimes. They also explain how to analyse the problem in a specific area and to develop solutions (http://www.popcenter.org).

- *Home Office (UK)* – This site contains information about terrorism, crime, antisocial behaviour, drugs and alcohol, as well as legislation, policies and procedures.

- *Crime Reduction Toolkits* – These toolkits contain advice on tackling issues, such as business crime and retail crime, vehicle crime, street crime and robbery, antisocial behaviour and fear of crime. There is also specific guidance on hospitals and schools and transport. The contents of the Crime Reduction website, including the toolkits, have been archived at: http://tna.europarchive.org/20100413151441/crimereduction.homeoffice.gov.uk/toolkits

- *European Standard for the Prevention of Crime* – This contains guidelines on methods for assessing the risk of crime and/or fear of crime and measures, procedures and processes aimed at reducing these risks. Design guidelines are given for specific types of environments to prevent or counteract different crime problems consistently with the urban planning documents. Furthermore, guidelines for a step-by-step process are presented to involve all stakeholders engaged in urban planning and environmental crime reduction as well as all other stakeholders, mainly local and regional authorities and residents, in the multi-agency action needed to minimise the risks of crime and fear of crime. The guidance is applicable to the planning process of new, as well as existing, urban areas.

The current standard was approved by the CEN, 21 July 2007. The reference is: CEN/TR 14383–2:2007:E. The document supersedes ENV 14383–2:200. The standard can be bought from http://shop.bsigroup.com/en.

The UK also produces planning policy documents, which are considered more specific to building developments in the UK.

Concept generation and design

Safety and security should be considered when generating design concepts. This involves identifying the potential crime scenarios and risk factors that relate to the proposed design solution – some of which may have been covered in the project objectives. For each design concept, the design team should consider the causal factors that may be acting in the identified crime scenarios. This may be undertaken using the *crime lifecycle model*, which is presented in the next chapter. Using creative thinking, crime prevention ideas can be generated that address the identified causal factors and crime scenarios. A single idea may successfully tackle multiple causal factors.

Feasibility testing and concept selection

Feasibility testing activities may occur concurrently with concept generation activities, in an iterative process. In most situations, feasibility testing is focused mainly on establishing the business case for a design concept (i.e. whether it can practically meet identified financial and resource-related targets).

The costs and benefits of safety and security will need to be evaluated. Care will need to be taken to ensure that crime prevention design features are not compromised at this stage, and Design Against Crime efforts sidelined.

Developing a business case

Information on the cost of crime has been published by Richard Dubourg and Joe Hamed in June 2005. The title of the report is 'Estimates of the Economic and Social Costs of Crime in England and Wales: Costs of Crime Against Individuals and Households, 2003/04'. The report is available from the Economics and Resource Analysis Research, Development and Statistics Home Office. In the 2005 report, the original estimates of the costs of crime against individuals and households, published in 2000 in Home Office Research Study 217, have been updated on the basis of methodological and data improvements. The report suggests that the cost of crime includes: costs in anticipation of crime; costs as a consequence of crime; and costs in response to crime (Dubourg & Hamed, 2005).

The total cost of crime against individuals and households in 2003–2004 was around £36.2 billion. The average cost varies considerably between different types of crime. The average cost of an incident was estimated as follows:

- Violence against the person – £10,407
- Sexual offences – £31,438
- Common assault – £1,440
- Robbery – £7,282
- Burglary in a dwelling – £3,268

- Theft (not a vehicle) – £634
- Theft of vehicle – £4,138
- Theft from vehicle – £858
- Criminal damage – £866.

Source: Dubourg and Hamed (2005), Table 2.1: Estimated average costs of crimes against individuals and households in 2003–2004 by crime type and by cost category.

Design testing and validation

Design testing and validation activities may occur concurrently with detailed design activities, in an iterative process. When the proposed design solution has passed the testing and validation process, the design can be said to be 'finished'. User and expert feedback will need to be obtained in relation to safety and security. Input may be sought from:

- Users, especially groups highlighted as being at risk
- Management and maintenance personnel
- Crime experts (e.g. local police, security personnel)
- Design-led crime prevention experts (e.g. police ALO).

The design solutions can be assessed in terms of compliance with guidance and standards, where relevant and available. Most importantly, the design should undergo a bench test or (better still) field trial of practical design measures, where possible. This is undertaken to check that physical design features will function reliably in a real-world environment. Advice on performance assessment may be given by crime prevention experts, and organisations such as the Home Office Scientific Development Branch (HOSDB). (For further details, see http://www.homeoffice.gov.uk/crimpol/police/scidev.)

It is important to consider potential countermeasures that may be taken by offenders in response to the design solution. The aim here is not to inadvertently make the crime situation worse, or cause an escalation of the crime risk. In addition, longer-term issues relating to the implementation and use of the design solution that may impact on the effectiveness of crime prevention aspects should be considered. As the design solution 'ages', or as users become more accustomed to it, its crime prevention attributes may become less effective or countermeasures developed. In some cases, this may be predicted, and addressed through management and maintenance activities.

Preparation for launch/handover

Launch/handover activities are concerned with communicating information about the design solution to its potential owners, users, managers and maintainers. It is important to ensure that appropriate information regarding crime prevention elements of the design solution are communicated – and in an appropriate manner. Care should be taken not to increase fear of crime unduly. Commercial issues may make communication of safety and security issues problematic. For example statements promoting a design's security may result in legal claims if the design later proves to be vulnerable.

In Phase 3 – use and performance

Management and maintenance

Management and maintenance activities are clearly relevant only to certain design areas, such as construction and the built environment. It is important to manage and maintain the design solution (and its crime prevention elements) appropriately. Management and maintenance problems or shortfalls that may relate to crime need to be recorded, the causes identified and problems resolved. For learning to occur, projects must be monitored and evaluated at regular intervals throughout their life. This involves considering how the design solution is performing with regards to crime prevention.

In Phase 4 – learning and business strategy

This activity is concerned with the transformation of experience into knowledge, and how such knowledge contributes to an organisation's learning and its future strategy. The business case for addressing safety and security will need to be reviewed, and findings incorporated into the business strategy. Based on the new strategy, changes will need to be made to methods for collecting data about market trends. Where relevant, crime and security issues should be covered within ongoing research, and the findings communicated to staff.

Further guidance on concept generation

Raising issues at the outset supports designers in their creative efforts to develop solutions to safety and security. Importantly, designers will need to incorporate their understanding of the risks and requirements into concept generation activities. This involves understanding offender motivations, perceptions and behaviours, and considering the causal factors that may be acting in potential crime scenarios. In the next chapter, we explain how to generate crime prevention strategies for the proposed design solution.

References

Clarke, R.V. (1999). 'Hot Products: Understanding, Anticipating and Reducing Demand for Stolen Goods'. Police Research Series Paper 112. London: Home Office Research, Development and Statistics Directorate. Downloaded from: http://www.popcenter. org/tools/risky_facilities/PDFs/Clarke_1999.pdf

Cooper, R.G. & Kleinschmidt, E.J. (1987) 'New Products: What Separates Winners from Losers?' *The Journal of Product Innovation Management*, Vol. 4, Iss. 3, pp. 167–184. http://onlinelibrary.wiley.com/doi/10.1111/1540-5885.430169/abstract

Cooper, R.G. and Kleinschmidt, E.J. (1995) 'New Product Performance: Keys to Success, Profitability & Cycle Time Reduction'. *Journal of Marketing Management*, Vol. 11, pp. 315–337.

CSEW. (2013a) 'Crime in England and Wales'. Year Ending March 2013. London: Office for National Statistics, Statistical Bulletin. Download full report from: http://www.ons.gov.uk/ons/dcp171778_318761.pdf

CSEW. (2013b) 'The Likelihood of Becoming a Victim of Crime'. Part of Crime Statistics, period ending March 2013 Release. London: Office for National Statistics. Released: 18 July. Download from: http://www.ons.gov.uk/ons/rel/crime-stats/crime-statistics/period-ending-march-2013/sty-a-victim-of-crime.html

Davey, C.L., Mackay, L. and Wootton, A.B. (2009) 'Designing Safe Residential Areas'. In R. Cooper, G. Evans and C. Boyko (eds.) *Designing Sustainable Cities*. Chichester, UK: Wiley-Blackwell.

Davey, C.L. and Wootton, A.B. (2010) *Design+Security & Crime Prevention. Enabling Socially Responsible Design by Embedding Security and Crime Prevention within the Design Process*. Salford, UK: University of Salford. Unpublished report for the UK Design Council.

Design Council. (2003) *Think Thief: A Designer's Guide to Designing Out Crime*. London: UK Design Council.

Dubourg, R. and Hamed, R. (2005) 'The Economic and Social Costs of Crime Against Individuals and Households 2003/04'. Home Office Online Report 30/05. Download from: http://webarchive.nationalarchives.gov.uk/20110218135832/rds.homeoffice.gov.uk/rds/pdfs05/rdsolr3005.pdf

Kleinschmidt, E.J. (1989) 'Success Factors in Product Innovation'. *Industrial Marketing Management*, Vol. 16, pp. 215–223.

Selwyn, N. (2009) 'Crime and Prejudice: Exploring the Victimisation of Undergraduate Students'. *International Review of Victimology*, January, Vol. 15, No. 3, pp. 205–222.

Wootton, A.B., Cooper, R. and Bruce, M. (1998) *A Generic Guide to Requirements Capture*. Salford, UK: University of Salford.

Wootton, A.B. and Davey, C.L. (2005) 'Design Against Crime Evaluation Framework. A Framework to support & Evaluate the Integration of Design Against Crime Within Development Projects'. Salford, UK: Design Against Crime Solution Centre, University of Salford.

Wootton, A.B., Marselle, M., Davey, C.L., Armitage, R. and Monchuk, L. (2009) 'National Police Crime Prevention Service. Implementation Planning Research Project'. Salford, UK: DAC Solution Centre. Available from: http://www.npcps.org

Wootton, A.B. and Davey, C.L. (2011) *'The Triple Diamond' in Design Council Designing Out Crime: A Designers' Guide Design Council*. London, UK: Design Council. pp. 99–100.

6 Concept generation and design
An offender-focused perspective

In order to develop strategies to reduce the vulnerability of a design to crime, the designer must consider the design from the perspective of the offender – that is to 'think thief'. This involves considering the perceptions, beliefs and emotions that frame an offender's decision-making immediately prior to committing an offence. This chapter presents a model created to help designers look at their design from the perspective of an offender in a structured way – the *Crime Lifecycle*. The insights and ideas generated from the use of this model enable designers to generate crime prevention concepts and strategies that address the 'causes of crime', and therefore reduce vulnerability. Such concepts and strategies can then be reviewed, and the best ones incorporated into the design solution.

Offender-centred model of crime

When thinking about the reasons individuals commit crime, it is tempting to focus on background causal factors that influence offenders. These occur sometime before any crime actually takes place, and include issues such as poverty, social deprivation, substance abuse and drug addiction.

However, as well as these background issues there exists a chain of other causal factors – conditions that have to be fulfilled – in the period leading up to and immediately before an offender commits a crime. These factors relate to the following:

- The offender
- The person, item or place that forms the focus for their criminal intent (usually referred to as the target)
- The environment in which the offence occurs.

By understanding these 'causal factors', and their relationship to offenders' thinking and behaviour, designers can develop measures to counter them. With creative thinking, designers can devise ways to reduce the risk of crime and antisocial behaviour without inconveniencing legitimate users – indeed, in many cases without their knowledge. Even the activities of highly motivated, 'professional' criminals can be restricted by well-considered design.

The crime lifecycle model

The aim of categorising the causal factors of crime is twofold:

- To enable a better understanding of the influences and choices affecting offender behaviour in a crime situation
- To enable these to be considered and (where possible) addressed in a systematic manner.

The crime lifecycle model (see Figure 6.1) is a design resource derived from a causal framework developed by criminologist Paul Ekblom whilst at the UK Home Office. Ekblom's (2001) original framework has been adapted and extended by the authors for use by design professionals in considering crime issues during the development of their design concepts (Wootton and Davey, 2003).

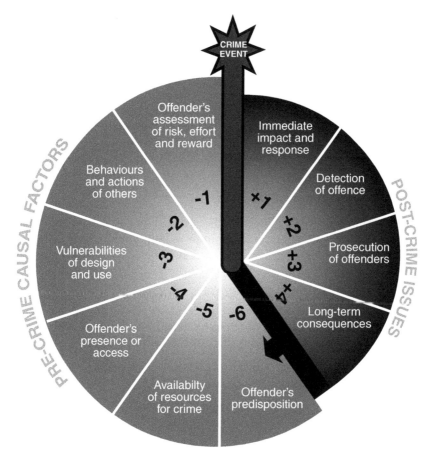

Figure 6.1 The crime lifecycle model.

Source: Davey & Wootton (2010).

The crime lifecycle model is organised into six pre-crime causal factors, which are numbered −6 to −1, and four post-crime issues, numbered +1 to +4. These ten causal factors and issues are pivoted around what is called the 'crime event' − that is the moment the offence takes place and a victim is created. The model embodies three key principles:

1   *Offending behaviour breeds further offending behaviour, so the real key to sustainable crime prevention is to break this cycle.*

The earliest (−6) and last (+4) phases of the model are linked. An offender's 'readiness to offend' is fuelled largely by his or her life circumstances and experiences − the extent to which the offender believes criminal behaviour to be acceptable and a valid option. In this way, the longer-term consequences of criminal activity impact on an offender's readiness to offend. For example the difficulties of finding employment experienced by those with a criminal record may encourage further criminal behaviour. In addition, being locked up with a large number of other criminals may provide an education in criminal skills and knowledge, and access to resources for future criminal activities.

2   *All six pre-crime causal factors (Phases −6 to −1) are prerequisite to a crime event occurring.*

By comprehensively addressing any one of these factors, the crime event can effectively be prevented from occurring. This means that designers do not necessarily have to tackle all of the pre-crime factors, but can choose to concentrate on the ones that can be most effectively addressed by design in their project.

3   *Post-crime issues should also be considered.*

It is unlikely that any design-led crime prevention measure will be 100 per cent effective. Therefore, it is useful to at least consider how issues arising after the crime event might be addressed by design. These post-crime issues are dealt with in Phases +1 to +4 of the lifecycle.

The remainder of this chapter will describe each phase of the crime lifecycle model (Figure 6.1) in sequence, starting with Phase −6 and ending with Phase +4. The model can be used by designers to better understand offender motivations and generate design solutions that reduce the risk of crime.

Pre-crime causal factors

−6: offender's predisposition

Offenders commit crimes because they believe their actions will be rewarded. The perceived reward is usually financial, but offences may also be driven by gains in reputation and status within their circle of friends and acquaintances.

This 'reward' element will be considered later, but this stage is interested in the predisposition of someone who would need and/or seek such reward. The likelihood of an individual turning to crime will be affected by his or her life history and circumstances, including the following:

- Financial situation
- Educational background
- Employment
- Family situation
- Sense of 'belonging'.

The motivation to offend is higher amongst young males and those from deprived backgrounds. Amongst these groups, offending is more socially acceptable while access to traditional jobs and careers is limited due, for example, to poor educational attainment and lack of business connections.

Design strategy

This is the most problematic phase of the crime lifecycle for designers to address, as it often relates to issues and decisions beyond the scope of their role. For example the predisposition to offend could be tackled by providing more opportunities for young people from deprived areas – including art projects, playgrounds and legitimate places for young people to 'hang out'. However, while such facilities are 'designed', the choice to deliver such projects is not usually made by designers but by the clients for whom they work (e.g. developers, housing associations, local authorities). Thus, such interventions are not really the result of design decisions *per se*.

   However, for designers of environments, there is a process-related strategy that can have an impact on the 'predisposition to offend' issue. Meaningful consultation on design issues with local people both enables a better understanding of issues facing deprived communities and encourages a sense of ownership of newly developed facilities. This increased sense of ownership can prevent vandalism and criminal damage, and thereby reduce feelings of insecurity. Good-quality housing and facilities designed to reduce crime and antisocial behaviour and promote positive interaction between neighbours can help regenerate problem areas. The nature of this causal factor makes it difficult to address through the design of products.

–5: availability of resources for crime

Offenders require resources to commit crime. The term 'resources' is a broad one, and can include the following:

- Tools and equipment (e.g. crowbar to open a window, a knife to threaten someone, a card 'skimmer' to steal credit card details)

- Knowledge and skills (e.g. a familiarity with the layout of a residential area, skill in picking locks, knowledge of CCTV blind spots)
- Co-offenders during the crime (e.g. someone to keep a lookout during a burglary or to help intimidate a victim in a mugging)
- Co-offenders after the crime (e.g. someone to buy stolen goods, someone to provide a false alibi). Everyday objects may be used as resources for crime – from shopping trolleys used by burglars to transport stolen goods, aerosol car paints used by vandals to cover walls in graffiti, to wheely bins used by burglars to help them climb over walls and fences. Products, services and systems may be put to use by offenders in ways never intended by their designers.

Design strategy

There are two main ways in which to think about this phase of the crime life cycle:

1 *Your design as the target of criminal resources*

   Consider the types of resources (tools, knowledge, skills) used by offenders to attack designs of the type that you are working on. How might your design render such resources of less value to potential offenders, or reduce their availability?

2 *Your design used/misused as a resource for crime*

   Consider how offenders make illegitimate use of designs of the type that you are working on. How might your design be made less useful for criminal purposes?

Design strategies to address these issues may include not only physical design features but also service and system design issues – how the design is purchased, used, managed, maintained and disposed of. Controlling tools and weapons as a means of preventing crime is recommended by researchers. Design can play a significant role in this. For example glass bottles may be used as weapons during fights, causing serious injury. In the past, waste bins containing bottles have been used as a source of weapons by drunk groups fighting in the street at night. To limit the availability of bottles on the street, waste bins have been designed and implemented that prevent bottles and other objects from being removed.

−4: offender's presence or access

Crime or conflict situations require the presence of or access by an offender. This may be:

- Purposeful (e.g. presence in a bank for a planned robbery)
- Opportunistic (e.g. presence in a crowded bar where someone leaves a mobile phone on a table).

Opportunistic crime as part of a daily routine

Offenders often take advantage of opportunities that arise during the course of their daily routine – this is called routine activity theory (Felson & Clarke, 1998). Such 'routine activity' may include travelling to work, visiting a friend's house or returning home. In the course of such activity, the offender may notice (and take advantage of) an opportunity for crime – an open window, a poorly secured bike, a satnav cradle in a parked car or a lone person using an expensive mobile phone.

As a result, many offenders tend to commit crimes near their homes, and offences are often concentrated around their everyday routes and so-called activity nodes, such as schools, workplaces, train stations and entertainment areas (Wiles & Costello, 2000). Consequently, buildings and facilities situated in busy locations may be at higher risk from crimes such as theft, burglary and vandalism.

Source: W. Bernasco & T. Kooistra (2010).

Design strategy and intervention examples

Designers should consider the following:

1   What are the potential crime and conflict situations that may occur in relation to their design?
2   How might their design reduce the likelihood of offenders being able to convert their presence or access in such situations into a crime?

The issue of offender access is most often addressed in environmental design by the technique known as target hardening. Most commonly, this involves introducing barriers – or levels of access control – to reduce the purposeful presence of potential offenders. One issue with this approach, however, is that target hardening can introduce a level of visual brutality that then increases fear of crime amongst legitimate users. Where possible, more subtle design solutions are preferable.

Physical vs psychological barriers

Visually, some physical barriers are clearly about 'security' – high fences, gates topped with razor wire and barred windows. While effective, they are not particularly attractive. Alleygates, for example, can be used to prevent access to the rear of properties – a common point of access to dwellings for burglars in the UK.

Other, potentially more attractive, options are available, however – including wide hedges, rose beds, lily ponds and reed beds. Within buildings, the placement and design of the reception area can help control access to the interior.

However, sometimes effective barriers can be simply psychological. At ATMs in Manchester, for example, a yellow privacy box is painted on the street to indicate that the area near the cash machine is for use only by the person using it – and that others in the queue should keep their distance.

The painted box acts as a psychological barrier to potential offenders, who generally do not want to be noticed looking over someone's shoulder at a cashpoint. It also makes it obvious to anyone watching when the personal space of a cashpoint user is being compromised.

However, this intervention relies on the presence of other legitimate users for it to work. Late at night, when there will likely be fewer people around, this psychological barrier may be less effective.

Figure 6.2 ATM privacy area (photograph by Mark Norman Francis).

–3: vulnerabilities of design and use

Offenders are choosy about what they steal, tending to focus on items that have high intrinsic value and/or can be easily sold on and turned into cash.

Products that are perceived by offenders as valuable and easy to remove and carry are more likely to be targeted.

An acronym has been developed to describe those products most often targeted by offenders – CRAVED. As outlined in Chapter 2, this stands for:

C – Concealable (easily hidden after theft; or theft not likely to be noticed initially)

R – Removable (easily taken, carried and transported – especially on the person)

A – Available (on display; or in an insecure location; or not being watched over)

V – Valuable (of significant monetary value, or signifying status or power)

E – Enjoyable (fun to use or possess, and therefore desirable)

D – Disposable (easily sold on or exchanged for cash, drugs, etc.)

However, offenders not only focus on the target but also are choosy about where they commit crimes. Places that are easily accessible, free from surveillance (by CCTV or other users) and easy to damage are most vulnerable to crime (Clarke & Eck, 2010).

Hot products

Cash is the most frequently stolen item in thefts, burglaries and robberies. It determines the location of many types of theft, including bank robberies, muggings near ATMs and thefts from ticket machines.

However, thieves also tend to target a relatively small number of so-called hot products, including cars, laptop computers, DVD players, satnavs and mobile phones. The items that fall within the hot product category do vary, however, depending on what is available and fashionable (Clark, 1999; Switched Staff, 2008).

Design strategy and intervention examples

Designers should consider:

- What are the vulnerable features of their design?
- How might the design of features, related services, user behaviours or the system within which the design exists reduce this vulnerability?

Reduce anonymity and identify products

Products that can be easily identified or have been personalised are less attractive to thieves, in part, because they are harder to sell. Methods for reducing anonymity include vehicle number plates, property marking and methods for personalising products.[1]

Reduce visibility of valuable products

Early methods of reducing theft of car stereos relied on users being willing to remove the entire stereo or carry the faceplate, which housed all the controls, with them whenever they left their car. Unfortunately, the user behaviour that emerged from the 'faceplate removal' design model was to remove the faceplate and simply put it in the glove compartment – negating any security benefit.

Recognising that users did not want to have to carry around any part of their car stereo, Kenwood designed its D Mask system so that the stereo could be hidden when not in use – thus reducing the chances of it being targeted by thieves while still meeting user requirements (see Figure 6.3).

The DIY example shown in Figure 6.4 is based on the same principle, except that this hides a modern CD player behind a fake ancient cassette player facia – which is much less likely to be targeted by thieves.

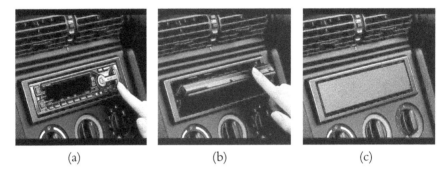

(a)   (b)   (c)

Figure 6.3a, 6.3b and 6.3c Kenwood D Mask car stereo system designed to be easily hidden.

Source: Design Council (2002). *Evidence Pack: DAC case studies.* London: Design Council. Available from http://www.designagainstcrime.org.uk/resources/DAC_Evidence_Pack.pdf

(a)   (b)

Figure 6.4a and 6.4b A modern car CD stereo system (left) is hidden behind a fake cassette player facia (right).

Source: http://www.instructables.com/id/Car-stereo-stock-radio-fake-out/ (CC license).

–2: behaviours and actions of others

In a crime situation, individuals can act as preventers or promoters. These can be:

- Active preventers – for example a police officer or a security guard
- Passive preventers – for example the mere presence of other people deterring an offender
- Careless promoters – for example someone leaving valuables on display in their parked car
- Deliberate promoters – for example an accomplice who keeps watch while his or her friend burgles a house, or someone who knowingly buys a stolen mobile phone.

Potential victims, as well as authorities such as the police or security guards, may fall into the first two of these categories. However, it is the third category – the user as careless promoter – that is especially valuable for designers to explore.

The way in which a product is designed to be used may actually put users at increased risk of victimisation if crime is not considered during design development. A common form of mobile phone theft – termed snatch theft – is enabled by the use of mobile phones while walking in the street. Offenders will approach distracted mobile phone users from behind, simply snatch the phone from their hand, and run off. Sometimes the offender may be riding a bicycle.

A study of crime data over the past two years in an area of Manchester city centre shows the vulnerability of this use design issue. When mobile phones stolen by stealth theft (pickpocketing) are excluded, snatch thefts account for almost three-quarters (73.7 per cent) of all remaining mobile phone thefts.

Where possible, appropriate design features should counter users inadvertently putting themselves at risk when using the designed product, service or system.

Personal space – the user weak spot

Generally, it seems we overestimate the security of our immediate surroundings – our so-called personal space – and items within it. This may be due to the strong sense of ownership we feel of the space surrounding our bodies, the invasion of which may provoke feelings of discomfort, anger or anxiety (Hall, 1966). Unsurprisingly, it is customary not to intrude into a stranger's personal space, and this has become what is known as a social norm. Social norms can be described as 'Customary rules of behaviour that coordinate our interactions with others' (Young, 2007).

The increase in use of personal electronic devices over the past decade means there are now rich pickings for criminals within users' personal space (e.g. mobile phones, organisers, smartphones, MP3 players). In addition, bags, purses, wallets, coats and jackets tend to inhabit this same area.

A problem that has emerged in bars and clubs is that people will put belongings down within arm's reach – for example a bag or mobile phone – but not pay full attention to it. Offenders will happily break social norms in such circumstances to steal personal property.

A survey conducted by home insurer Direct Line suggests that in the UK, over a fifth of women (21 per cent) admit they have been the victim of bag theft. The top locations for this are, first, 'in the pub' (14 per cent) and second, 'in a club', 'out shopping' and 'at work' (at 12 per cent each) (Directline, 2009).

A study of crime data over the past two years in an area of Manchester city centre highlights the vulnerability of personal space. For the offence of miscellaneous theft, nearly half of all incidents (47.8 per cent) involved theft from or of a handbag, while more than a quarter of all offences (25.9 per cent) involved theft of property that was left on display by the victim – usually within the victim's personal space (Davey, Wootton & Marselle, 2011).

Source: Hall, Edward T. (1966) *The Hidden Dimension*. Anchor Books

The New Palgrave Dictionary of Economics, Second Edition, 2008.

Opinion Research carried out an online poll of 2,187 British adults during 20–24 February 2009. Further details available from www.directline.com/about_us/news_170409.htm

Davey, C.L., Wootton, A.B. and Marselle, M. (2011) Findings of Locality-Specific Surveys. United Kingdom, in *Planning Urban Security (PLuS): Interim Report* for European Commission–funded project, PLuS. For further details, visit www.plus-eu.net.

Design strategy and intervention examples

Designers should consider the following:

- Who are the potential preventers and who are the potential promoters that might impact on your design – including the user?
- How might your design support the actions and abilities of preventers, and reduce those of promoters? Design solutions that promote security should not be inconvenient – indeed, they need to be easy to use and ideally be more convenient than current services or products. Centralised locking, for example, makes it more convenient for car drivers to lock up when leaving the car while also reducing the risk that a door (or the boot) is accidentally left unlocked.

Design in low-risk user behaviour, or features to mitigate risk

Consider the way in which your product, system or environment is used in relation to the common methods and MOs employed to attack similar designs. Are there ways to render common MO types ineffective, or to alter users' behaviour to reduce their exposure to risk? Can your design prevent careless promotors or encourage the passive preventer role? Clearly, this needs to be done without reducing the value of the design to legitimate users – which is where creative design thinking is required.

Parking stands – supporting better locking

Design can encourage users to be careful. Research in London suggests that bike thefts often occur because the bicycle has not been locked securely. The British Crime Survey estimates that in 2006/7 there were 482,000 'thefts of a pedal cycle' in the UK. The total economic and social cost was estimated to be in the region of £260 million per annum. Twenty-four per cent of victims do not replace the bicycle and 66 per cent cycle less often – thus undermining efforts to promote sustainable transport. In the 'Bike Off' project led by Central Saint Martins to design more secure parking stands, Broxap Ltd prototyped six stands that increase the percentage of people locking their bikes securely. The 'M Stand', for example, encourages cyclists to lock both the wheel and metal frame to the stand.

Figure 6.5 M Stand on the street (photograph by Design Against Crime Research Centre, UAL in Arts and Humanities Research Council, 2008).

–1 Offender's assessment of risk, effort and reward

This phase concerns the period immediately before the crime is committed. This is when the offender decides whether the risk and effort are worth the potential reward. Consequently, increasing the offender's perception of risk and effort and reducing that of reward will affect the offender's decision-making, thus potentially preventing the offence. Methods for achieving this include the following:

- Increasing the offender's perceived risk of detection and subsequent identification
- Increasing the amount of effort required by the offender to gain the reward
- Reducing the perceived reward the offence offers; this may be financial, but is likely to include other factors that motivate the offender (e.g. increased status in his or her peer group).

Design strategy and intervention examples

Increase perceived risk of detection and identification

Risk of detection and risk of identification are significant de-motivators for offenders. The questions they ask themselves just before committing an offence are:

1   Can I be seen?
2   If I am seen, will I be noticed?
3   If I am seen and noticed, will anybody do anything about it?

Designing in features that are likely to make a potential offender answer 'yes' to any of these questions has the potential to prevent crime.

Increase perceived effort required

Designers should investigate the MOs used to commit crimes likely to be used against their design or its users. They should then consider how such criminal efforts might be made more difficult for the offender, including the following:

- Increasing the effort required for offenders to avoid detection
- Increasing the effort required for offenders to access the target
- Increasing the effort required for offenders to leave the scene after the offence (often, with the target).

Such design measures are as much about manipulating an offender's perception of the effort required as about adding countermeasures for the offender's methods of attack. For example there will be a time factor in any criminal attack, with risk for the offender increasing the longer it takes him or her to access the target. For this reason, doors designed to meet the Police Secured by Design standard (BSI PAS 24) are attack-proof for a specified time, rather than impregnable. The majority of offenders are opportunistic, and research has shown that after a certain time they will simply give up and move on.

Vandalism – reducing the buzz factor

Some forms of vandalism are linked to this 'buzz' factor. For example some bus shelters are targeted by vandals who enjoy the spectacle and exhilaration resulting from large toughened glass panels breaking into tiny pieces and crashing to the ground when struck with a hard object. Such a noisy display also offers a means for offenders to 'impress' their peers, thereby providing further motivation for their act of vandalism.

Simply laminating such panels with clear plastic film prevents this aesthetic effect, thus removing a significant reward for the offender.

In a similar way, quickly cleaning away graffiti prevents vandals from being able to gain status or recognition from their activities.

Figure 6.6 Smashing fun in bus shelters

Source: Design Council (2002). Evidence Pack: DAC case studies. London: Design Council. Available from http://www.designagainstcrime.org.uk/resources/DAC_Evidence_Pack.pdf

Reduce perceived reward

Finally, understanding the way in which offenders derive 'reward' from their offending behaviour may reveal ways in which design can reduce this motivation. Such reward may be solely monetary (e.g. the resale value of a stolen mobile phone), but may also include other factors. These may be external factors, such as increased status in their peer group, or internal ones, such as a feeling of excitement or exhilaration, sometimes referred to as a 'buzz'.

Reducing the reward of criminal activities is a proven method for preventing crime. Designers should think about how they might disrupt the criminal value chain, which means understanding how the offender derives value or reward from the offence. A simple example is given here:

A product is designed to be easily identifiable if it is stolen
So . . .
It is more difficult for criminals to dispose of / sell the stolen product
So . . .
It is less easy for criminals to convert the product into cash
So . . .
The product is less attractive to criminals
So . . .
Theft of the product (and risk of legitimate users becoming victims of theft) falls.

Not all crime can be prevented, so designers should also consider issues arising after a crime has been committed.

Post-crime issues

+1: immediate impact and response

The immediate actions of a victim or offender in the moments after a crime has been committed can affect the following:

- The likelihood of intervention by a third party
- The likelihood of the offender being identified, caught and prosecuted
- The physical and emotional impact on the victim
- The psychological impact on the offender
- The potential for the crime to escalate.

The impact of the crime depends to some extent on the MO used by the offender. For example the four most common bag theft techniques – dip, snatch, lift and slash – will have different effects on the victim. Dipping (also known as pickpocketing) involves discrete access gained through a bag or pocket and generally goes unnoticed by the victim, who only later realises that valuables are missing. Snatching (also known as 'grabbing') is defined as theft from person, unless force is used, when the crime is classified as robbery.

In this case, the potential for physical and emotional harm to the victim is much higher.

Design strategy and intervention examples

The potential negative impact of design attributes intended to address pre-crime causal factors should be considered, to ensure that the immediate impact for the victim is not inadvertently made worse. This might cause the crime to escalate. For example while strengthening the strap on a bag might reduce the risk of the bag being snatched, it might also result in the wearer being dragged along by an offender or being subjected to a level of force resulting in injury.

Karrysafe bags – not to die for

Vexed Generation and Central Saint Martins College of Art & Design collaborated in the development of Karrysafe – a range of bags designed to fight the four most common bag theft techniques: dip, snatch, lift and slash.

Figure 6.7 The Karrysafe bag (photograph by Design Against Crime Research Centre, UAL. www.inthebag.org.uk/?page_id=479).

What makes the bags considerably safer than standard ones are built-in features like the 'Screamer'. This anti-attack alarm for laptop bags starts screaming if the bag is taken from you by force. The screamer forces the offender to dump the bag. The user follows from a safe distance, and simply picks up the discarded bag. The screamer encourages the victim to let go of the bag, which reduces the risk of being harmed. Indeed, police advise victims to hand over valuables if threatened or attacked:

> **'If someone tries to take something from you by force, it may be best to give it to them. This will help you avoid getting injured.'**
>
> −City of London Police

Source: www.treehugger.com/files/2007/01/karrysafe_bags.php and www.cityof london.police.uk/CityPolice/Advice/personalsafety/theft.htm

+2: detection of offence

An offence may be detected during or after its occurrence by the following:

- Witnesses (e.g. residents, passers-by, police, security guards)
- Technological systems (e.g. alarms sounding, viewing on CCTV)
- The victims themselves (e.g. detecting the pickpocket, hearing the intruder, noticing their mobile phone has gone).

Knowing that an offence has taken place can prevent more serious harm. For example a customer being able to detect whether packaged food has been tampered with, or knowing that your wallet containing credit and bank cards has been stolen before they are used to empty your bank account.

Design strategy and intervention examples

Designers should consider the following:

- How might their design (or the system within which the design exists) enable the early detection of offences?
- How might their design communicate (or provide evidence) that an offence has taken place?

Detecting deviations from the norm

To help protect customers and themselves from fraud, Barclaycard keeps an eye on members' accounts. So if they notice a transaction that seems out of the ordinary, they call the card holder as soon as possible to check it's legitimate. This system comprises an automated service that will call the user and ask him or her to verify that the user is a Barclaycard customer. The user is asked to verify the most recent transactions, and if there are any the user doesn't recognise, he or she can be put through to a fraud advisor. Credit card systems are designed to detect use that deviates from normal in terms of amounts spent, location of purchases and other factors.

Source: www.barclaycard.co.uk/personal-home/credit-guidance/fraud-guide/fraud_prevention_service/index.html

+3: prosecution of offenders

To successfully prosecute the offender, as well as any co-offenders, the authorities require the following:

- Robust witness testimony
- Valid physical evidence.

It is possible that design features (or features of the system within which the design exists) would help address this issue.

Design strategy and intervention examples

Designers should consider how their design might support witness testimony and the provision of valid physical evidence – including evidence that the design has been involved in a crime (e.g. that it is stolen).

There are a range of methods for identifying property, including proprietary marking liquids, like SmartWater (see box ahead), special dyes, ultraviolet (UV) markers, electronic identifying codes and registration numbers (e.g. car number plates).

There are also an increasing number of electronic identification technologies available that can detect and record the biometric data of users, including laptops and USB flash memory drives. Indeed, Apple has outlined the design of a system to detect unauthorised users who attempt to access an iPhone or other device. The system would identify legitimate users through a picture, the sound of their voice, or even their unique heartbeat. If unauthorised access is detected, the actual owner of the handset could be notified in a variety of manners, including a phone call, text message or e-mail. The system could even send the owner – or the police – a picture of the unauthorised user, or other information specific to the potential thief, such as the device's current location.

SmartWater aids sentencing of cash robbery gang

Forensic evidence provided by SmartWater resulted in the jailing of six men, including a 16-year-old youth, for two cash-in-transit robberies that took place in North East London in August 2009.

Dye-stained cash found on suspected offenders was found to contain a SmartWater forensic signature. This along with a piece of dye-stained newspaper recovered from their car was sent away for analysis at Smart-Water's laboratories. SmartWater scientists positively identified the dye as coming from a separate cash box stolen during a cash-in-transit robbery in Tottenham the previous day. This additional evidence played a key role in the severity of the gang's sentencing.

A Metropolitan Police Service spokesman said:

'These were dangerous individuals who posed a serious threat to the community and who could have been able to commit further offences had they not been apprehended.'

–DCI Ian Corner, Barking Flying Squad

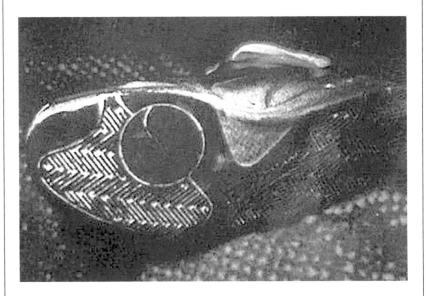

Figure 6.8 SmartWater.

Source: www.smartwater.com/Media-Centre/Latest-News-2/September-2010/SmartWater-aids-sentencing-of-cash-robbery-gang.aspx

+4: long-term consequences

Crime has longer-term effects on:

- Victims and their families
- Offenders and co-offenders
- The designed product or place involved in the offence
- Communities
- Wider society.

As mentioned earlier, these long-term consequences contribute to repeat offending and the emergence of the cycle of crime. As such they can reinforce an offender's predisposition – pre-crime causal factor –6.

Design strategy and intervention examples

As with Phase –6 of the crime life cycle, this longer-term causal factor is difficult for designers to address alone – especially through the design of products. However, if designers are looking to tackle this issue, they should consider the following:

- What are the longer-term consequences of crimes related to the design?
- How might the design (or features of the system within which the design exists) alleviate the negative effects of these?

Local authorities, criminal justice agencies and other organisations dealing with these longer-term issues can benefit greatly from the creative analysis, insight and innovative thinking of designers in addressing these difficult issues.

The next chapters outline practical examples of where crime and related social issues have been addressed using a design approach, including in education and the built environment.

References

Arts and Humanities Research Council (2008) 'Fighting Crime Through More Effective Design'. Brochure. AHRC, Bristol. Download from: http://www.designagainstcrime. com/files/Fighting%20crime%20through%20more%20effective%20design%20-%20 case%20study.pdf

Bernasco, W. and Kooistra, T. (2010) 'Effects of Residential History on Commercial Robbers' Crime Location Choices'. *European Journal of Criminology*, Vol. 7, No. 4, pp. 251–265.

Clarke, R.V. (1999) 'Hot Products: Understanding, Anticipating and Reducing Demand for Stolen Goods'. Police Research Series Paper 112. London: Home Office Research, Development and Statistics Directorate.

Clarke, R. and Eck, J. (2010) 'Know the Products That Are CRAVED by Thieves, Step Number 31'. Crime Analysis for Problem Solvers in 60 Small Steps. Center for Problem-Oriented Policing.

Davey, C.L. and Wootton, A.B. (2010) *Design+Security & Crime Prevention. Enabling Socially Responsible Design by Embedding Security and Crime Prevention within the Design Process.* Salford, UK: University of Salford. Unpublished report for the UK Design Council.

Davey, C.L., Wootton, A.B. and Marselle, M. (2011) Findings of Locality-Specific Surveys, United Kingdom, in Planning Urban Security (PLuS): Interim Report for European Commission–funded project, PLuS. Download from: http://www.lka.polizei-nds.de/praevention/vorbeugung_themen_und_tipps/staedtebau/staedtebau-152.html

Directline (2009) Opinion Research report of 2,187 British, 20–24 Feb 2009. Download from: http://www.directline.com/about_us/news_170409.htm

Durlauf, S.N and Blume, L.E. (Eds) (2008) *The New Palgrave Dictionary of Economics.* Second Edition. Download from: http://www.dictionaryofeconomics.com

Ekblom, P. (2001) 'Crime Reduction: The Conjunction of Criminal Opportunity'. Home Office Crime Reduction Toolkits. Download from: http://www.crimereduction.gov.uk/cco.htm

Felson, M. and Clarke, R.V. (1998) 'Opportunity Makes the Thief: Practical Theory for Crime Prevention'. Police Research Series Paper 98. London: Home Office Research, Development and Statistics Directorate.

Hall, E.T. (1966) 'The Hidden Dimension'. New York: Anchor Books. Download from: http://www.philo-online.com/TEXTES/HALL%20Edward%20Twichell%20-%20The%20hidden%20dimension.pdf

Switched Staff. (2008) '5 Most Stolen Gadgets'. 31 January. Download from: http://www.switched.com/2008/01/31/five-most-stolen-gadgets-2/

Wiles, P. and Costello, A. (2000) 'The 'Road to Nowhere': The Evidence for Travelling Criminals'. Home Office Research Study 207. London: Home Office Research, Development and Statistics Directorate.

Wootton, A.B. and Davey, C.L. (2003) *Crime Lifecycle: Guidance for Generating Design Against Crime Ideas.* Salford, UK: University of Salford.

Young, H.P. (2007) 'Social Norms'. Department of Economics Discussion Paper, number 309, January 2007. Oxford:University of Oxford. Download from: http://www.cs.uu.nl/docs/vakken/mas/papers/Young.pdf

Website

In the Bag, project led by Central Saint Martins College of Art & Design. Further information on perpetrator techniques is available from http://www.inthebag.org.uk/?page_id=225

Part III

Using design to address crime and security issues

7 Crime prevention policy

Crime has traditionally been dealt with by focusing on punishing the offender. Indeed, higher crime levels are often met with calls for harsher punishment. However, this strategy can be costly and does not necessarily result in lower crime levels. As Victorian social thinker and philanthropist John Ruskin points out, 'Punishment is the last and the least effective instrument in the hands of the legislator for the prevention of crime' (Ruskin, 1868). In the 2013 article 'The Curious Case of the Fall in Crime', *The Economist* announced, 'Crime is plunging in the rich world. To keep it down, governments should focus on prevention not punishment' (p. 9).

This chapter provides an overview of crime prevention approaches, before presenting in more detail the situational crime approach, including crime prevention through environmental design (CPTED). The urban environment has been the focus for crime prevention in the United States and across Europe.

The criminal justice system

The criminal justice system covers the police, crown courts, Crown Prosecution Service (CPS), prisons and probation service. In 2013, the UK spent £5.63

Table 7.1 Amount of money spent by UK government on different areas.

Area of expenditure	Actual spend (£ billion)
Interest payments on the national debt	48.2
Health	106.66
Working age benefits (e.g. tax credits and job seeker's allowance)	82
Defence	37.25
Overseas aid	7.87
State pensions	74.22
Education and schools (not including universities)	51.54
Policing and criminal justice	5.63
Transport	12.37
Base: 1,015 British adults aged 16–75	

Source: Ipsos MORI Perils of Perception. Topline Results. Fieldwork: 14–18 June 2013.

billion on policing and criminal justice (see Table 7.1). This compares with £106.66 billion on health (Ipsos MORI, 2013).

Despite the relatively low amount relative to other areas of public spending, crime and security are important topics for all political parties in the UK, as they seek to win over the public to their beliefs, policies and future plans.

The politics of crime and punishment

In the UK, those on the political right are more likely to blame criminal behaviour on factors related to the individual, including defects in 'moral character' and poor parenting, and to advocate tough punishment for offenders. In contrast, the left has traditionally blamed offending behaviour on societal causes, such as poverty and social deprivation, preferring to focus on improving social conditions for citizens and offender rehabilitation rather than on punishment (Pease, 2001; Waiton, 2006).

The divide between the political left and right in terms of their approach to crime has closed somewhat over 20 years. This was exemplified by the Labour Party slogan 'Tough on crime, tough on the causes of crime' (Tony Blair, British Prime Minister). As a result, over recent years we have seen a greater tendency to apportion blame for crime and security problems to parents and young people (hence references to 'yob culture'), to criminalise a wider range of behaviours and to focus on harsher sentencing and treatment – especially for young people (Waiton, 2006).

The UK's punitive approach to crime and disorder has resulted in a relatively large prison population compared to other European countries (Walmsley, 2012). In England and Wales, there are 148 prison inmates per 100,000 of national population, compared with 98 in France, 79 in Germany and 82 in the Netherlands (Walmsley, 2012, p. 5). However, threat of punishment may be of limited value in changing offending behaviour. In his review of the evidence on the deterrent effect, Raymond Paternoster suggests, 'Very little relationship may exist between people's estimates of the certainty and severity of punishment and their behavior' (Paternoster, 1987, p. 214). Another limitation of punishment as a tool for crime prevention is the fact that it affects only a small proportion of offenders. The number of offenders that are arrested, tried and convicted is extremely low for more common crime. In her inaugural speech, Professor Gloria Laycock (2001), of the Jill Dando Crime Science Institute, pointed out that only 2 per cent of offences result in conviction. Furthermore, punishment is expensive. For the UK, the average yearly cost of prison in 2010–11 was £37,163 per prisoner, while the cost for each young person between 15 and 17 years old in a young offenders institution was £76,913 (Ministry of Justice, 2011, p. 4).

Reoffending rates suggest that the experience of prison is of limited value in discouraging future criminality. Data on reoffending collected by the UK Ministry of Justice shows the following (Ministry of Justice, 2013):

- Fifty-eight per cent of adult prisoners released after less than 12 months' custody reoffended in the following 12 months.

- Thirty-five per cent of prisoners released after 12 months or more in custody reoffended in the following 12 months.

Countries or states that imprison a large proportion of the population do not achieve significantly lower levels of crime. In addition, there is a tendency for punitive measures to be applied more frequently to offenders from deprived, ethnic minority or immigrant communities. In his article 'Immigration, Crime and Unsafety', Hans-Jörg Albrecht (2002) concludes that newly arrived immigrants are considered differently to other groups of offenders, and are less likely to be considered suitable for alternatives to detention and imprisonment. This contributes to the fact that newly arrived immigrants make up a large proportion of the prison population.

However, the biggest drawback to relying on punishment to prevent crime is a human-centred one. Punishment necessarily occurs *after* an offence has taken place and in that sense is a post-victimisation measure – it is focused on catching offenders rather than reducing victimisation. Crime prevention focuses on preventing crimes from being committed in the first place. So what do we mean by crime prevention?

Crime prevention strategies

Problems of crime and insecurity in local neighbourhoods may lead to a demand for uniformed police officers. In the UK, the general public often demands 'more bobbies on the beat'. However, a police officer is unlikely to be present at the point when an individual is considering offending. The preventative value of uniformed officers patrolling the streets is therefore questionable. In addition, police presence may heighten awareness of crime problems, fuelling feelings of insecurity amongst local people. Crime prevention is not about police presence to deter criminal behaviour, but about a range of interventions focused on childhood and the environment. Crime prevention extends responsibility beyond the police to a range of stakeholders, including local authorities, social workers, planners, designers, developers and businesses.

Crime prevention strategies intervene before a crime occurs to reduce the chances of an offence being committed. Of course the time before a crime occurs is potentially very long. In addressing this period, there are two main approaches:

1   Focusing on the development of the potential offender, and intervening at an early stage to prevent him or her becoming criminalised
2   Focusing on the situation in which the offence is likely to occur, and intervening to change offender or potential victim behaviour.

Early intervention

Examples of early intervention include the provision of social programmes for children exposed to risk factors, such as parental neglect, poverty or social deprivation. In the criminology literature, such measures are referred to as 'early intervention'. They seek to address the deep-rooted causes of crime that impact on personality, behaviour, motivations, educational aptitude, relationships and so on, and thus on propensity to engage in offending behaviour.

Some interventions are focused on a later stage of development, including young people. Interventions may be focused on children or young people identified as 'at risk' of offending by, for example, the police, social workers and schools. Antisocial behaviour is a factor associated with offending for some young people, and early intervention is therefore recommended. 'In some cases, early intervention that targets young people involved in anti-social behaviour may help to reduce the likelihood of offending later on' (Hales *et al.*, 2009, p. i). Not all interventions are targeted at children and young people with problems or at risk of offending. Some interventions seek to engage a cross section of children or adults, perhaps focusing on a specific community or neighbourhood. This may be motivated by a desire to engage children and young people in shaping their own destiny (Hart, 1992). This has been the focus of youth development, public policy and social change movements for at least 40 years (Day *et al.*, 2011).

Some interventions make use of the creative design process to engage with children and young people identified as being at risk of offending by authorities (Condon, 2008). Such approaches can improve self-confidence and provide transferable skills, such as problem-solving, to young people who would otherwise leave full-time education with no qualifications (see Chapter 9 for more on this). However, the number of interventions of this kind is limited (Day *et al.*, 2011).

Interventions during the early years can bring about benefits in terms of reduced tendency to offend. The criminologist David Farrington, winner of the 2012 Stockholm Prize in Criminology, highlighted the large body of scientific evidence demonstrating the benefits of early intervention. Of course, a wide range of interventions have been delivered, including: efforts to lift families out of poverty, increase in kindergarten places in deprived areas and provision of parenting courses teaching proven strategies for child rearing. However, some types of intervention have been found to be unhelpful – some even making matters worse. For example there is no clear evidence that the idea of the 'short, sharp shock' and so-called boot camps for young offenders prevent offending behaviour (Wilson, 2005). There is, however, some evidence that such interventions can be harmful. For example a 2001 *New York Times* article highlighted that there had been 31 known deaths of youths in US boot camps since 1980 (Janofsky, 2001). One problem is that intervention measures often become political ammunition. Thus, in some countries measures that may be portrayed as 'soft' are equated with political weakness, regardless of their evidenced effectiveness at reducing offending behaviour. The popular call for harsh punishment can be a difficult one for political decision-makers to ignore, whatever the evidence for the ineffectiveness of such approaches.

Situational interventions

This approach to crime prevention focuses on the situation encountered by potential offenders and their victims immediately prior to an offence being committed – that is the point at which potential offenders are making decisions about offending. The aim is to increase the perceived risks and effort associated with the offending behaviour, or to reduce the perceived rewards. Interventions seek to reduce opportunities for crime through the design of the physical and social environment – buildings, products, services, processes, user behaviours, social norms and so on. This 'situational approach' is embodied within a range of practical crime prevention theories, including crime prevention through environmental design (CPTED) and situational crime prevention (SCP) – sometimes termed 'designing out crime' in Europe.

SCP draws on opportunity theory, as described in Chapter 2. Experts in the field demonstrate how easy opportunities tempt individuals into offending behaviour, and a proportion will commit further, more serious offences. Opportunity can be treated as a causal factor in crime (Farrell, 2013; Felson & Clarke, 1998). Consequently, efforts should be made to reduce victimisation, and organisations that generate opportunities for offending held to account.

Crime prevention through environmental design

Within the urban environment, crime, antisocial behaviour and insecurity are generally addressed using an approach termed Crime Prevention Through Environmental Design (CPTED). Formulated in the United States in the 1970s, CPTED aims to design out crime from the urban environment, and has been implemented to varying degrees across the world. In the UK, Home Office research focused on the decision-making approach of criminals, resulting in SCP theory being adopted in the 1980s (Cozens *et al.*, 2005).

Applied research has established design principles and practices for urban security relating to aspects such as natural surveillance, access control, sense of ownership and management and maintenance (Cozens *et al.*, 2005). These principles are commonly illustrated with examples of good practice from specific development projects.

Applying CPTED

The urban environment has been the focus for crime prevention. In Chapter 8, we discuss the application of crime prevention to urban design and planning across Europe. Design, planning and crime prevention policies play a key role in defining the extent to which architects consider safety and security for users of the buildings and environments they design.

References

Albrecht, H.-J. (2002) 'Immigration, Crime and Unsafety'. In A. Crawford (ed.) *Crime and Insecurity: The Governance of Safety in Europe*. Cullompton, UK: Willan, Chapter 6, pp. 159–185.

Condon, P.M. (2008) *Design Charrettes for Sustainable Communities*. Washington, DC: Island Press.

Cozens, P.M., Saville, G. and Hillier, D. (2005) 'Crime Prevention Through Environmental Design (CPTED): A Review and Modern Bibliography'. *Property Management*, Vol. 23, No. 5, pp. 328–356.

Day, L., Sutton, L. and Jenkins, S. (2011) 'Children and Young People's Participation in Planning and Regeneration'. A Final Report to the Ecorys Research Programme 2010–11. Birmingham, UK: Ecorys. Download from: http://www.uk.ecorys.com/news/april2011/children-young-people-report.html

The Economist. (2013) 'The Curious Case of the Fall in Crime'. *Leaders, The Economist*, 20 July. Download from: http://www.economist.com/news/leaders/21582004-crime-plunging-rich-world-keep-it-down-governments-should-focus-prevention-not

Farrell, G. (2013) 'Five Tests for a Theory of the Crime Drop'. Paper presented at International Symposium on Environmental Criminology and Crime Analysis (ECCA), Philadelphia, PA.

Felson, M. and Clarke, R.V. (1998) 'Opportunity Makes the Thief: Practical Theory for Crime Prevention'. Police Research Paper 98. London: Home Office.

Hales, J., Nevill, C., Pudney, S. and Tipping, S. (2009) 'Longitudinal Analysis of the Offending, Crime and Justices Survey, 2003–06. Key Implications'. Research Report 19, Home Office, November. ISBN 978–1–84987–100–6. Download from: http://webarchive.nationalarchives.gov.uk/20110218135832/rds.homeoffice.gov.uk/rds/pdfs09/horr19c.pdf

Hart, R.A. (1992) *Children's Participation: From Tokenism to Citizenship*. Florence, Italy: UNICEF.

Ipsos MORI (2013) 'Ipsos MORI Perils of Perception. Topline Results. Fieldwork: 14th–18th June 2013'. Ipsos MORI, London. Download from: https://www.ipsos-mori.com/Assets/Docs/Polls/ipsos-mori-rss-kings-perils-of-perception-topline.pdf

Janofsky, M. (2001) 'States Pressed as 3 Boys Die at Boot Camps'. *New York Times*, 15 July.

Laycock, G. (2001) 'Scientists or Politicians – Who Has the Answer to Crime?'. London: Jill Dando Institute of Crime Science School of Public Policy, University College London. Unabridged version of lecture delivered 26 April. Download from: http://www.ucl.ac.uk/scs/about-us/tabbed-box/Prof-Laycock-Inaugural-Lecture

Ministry of Justice. (2011) 'Costs per Place and Costs per Prisoner by Individual Prison – National Offender Management Service Annual Report and Accounts 2010–11: Management Information Addendum'. Ministry of Justice Information Release, 27 October.

Ministry of Justice. (2013) 'Transforming Rehabilitation: A Summary of Evidence on Reducing Reoffending'. Ministry of Justice Analytical Series. Download from: https://www.gov.uk/government/uploads/system/uploads/attachment_data/file/243718/evidence-reduce-reoffending.pdf

Paternoster, R. (1987) 'The Deterrent Effect of the Perceived Certainty and Severity of Punishment – A Review of the Evidence and Issues'. *Justice Quarterly*, Vol. 4, No. 2, pp. 173–217, doi:10.1080/07418828700089271

Pease, K. (2001) *Cracking Crime Through Design*. London: Design Council.

Ruskin, J. (1868) *Notes on the General Principles of Employment for the Destitute and Criminal Classes*. London: Strangeways and Walden.

Waiton, S. (2006) 'Anti-social Behaviour: The Construction of a Crime'. January 19, *Spiked*. Downloaded from: http://www.spiked-online.com/newsite/article/5#.V_y27hSAS9o

Walmsley, R. (2012) *World Prison Population List*. Tenth edn. London: International Centre for Prison Studies, University of Essex.

Wilson, D.B, MacKenzie D.L. and Mitchell F.N. (2005) 'Effects of Correctional Boot Camps on Offending'. *Campbell Systematic Reviews*, Vol. 1, No. 6, doi: 10.4073/csr.2005.6. Download from: http://www.campbellcollaboration.org/library.html

8 Crime prevention in European urban design and planning

Within Europe, crime prevention policies have primarily focused on the design of the physical urban environment. For example in the UK steps have been taken to embed crime prevention into policing, planning policies, architectural design practice and urban management. These steps have been supported by government legislation to make public bodies formally responsible for reducing the vulnerability of citizens to crime – with consequent implications for architects, developers and planners. While this approach has been successful, there are arguments that its future efficacy is being undermined by public spending cuts and changes in government policy to reduce so-called red tape. As this chapter goes on to discuss, other European countries are also addressing crime through urban design and planning.

Crime prevention through environmental design

In relation to the urban environment, design, planning and crime prevention policies and practices play a key role in defining the extent to which architects consider safety and security for users of the buildings and environments they design. As discussed in the previous chapter, crime, antisocial behaviour and insecurity are generally addressed using an approach termed Crime Prevention Through Environmental Design (CPTED). In the UK, this approach is often referred to as designing out crime (Cozens *et al.*, 2005). As this chapter explains, CPTED has been widely applied in the UK, largely through support from legislation, police and local authorities.

United Kingdom – policy and practice

In the UK, local authorities are under pressure to consider crime issues. Section 17 of the 1998 Crime and Disorder Act (Great Britain, 1998) states that:

> It is the duty of the authority to exercise its various functions with due regard to the likely effect of the exercise on crime and disorder in its area, and the need to do all that it reasonably can to prevent crime and disorder in its area.

While the wording is relatively vague, the result was that local authorities and providers of public services were all made aware of their responsibility to prevent crime and disorder. Following on from the act, Crime and Disorder Reduction Partnerships (CDRP) were established. These brought together police, local authorities (including planners and city managers), fire services, health authorities, public transport services, registered social landlords (e.g. housing associations), the voluntary sector, businesses and local residents. These different stakeholders work together collaboratively to tackle problems of crime and antisocial behaviour within the region. In 2010, CDRPs were renamed Community Safety Partnerships (Home Office, 2010). Police performance was judged on public confidence. This has contributed to an increased focus on fear of crime and feelings of insecurity (Barker & Crawford, 2006–2009), which can be linked to concerns over low-level crime, such as antisocial behaviour. Since 1998, the UK has seen the introduction of policies focusing on antisocial behaviour (ASB). This is defined as 'Acting in a manner that caused or was likely to cause harassment, alarm or distress to one or more persons not of the same household as [the defendant]' (Crime & Disorder Act, Great Britain, 1998).

ASB covers a whole range of acts, from substance misuse to kerb crawling, excess noise, drinking on the street and behaviour which is rowdy and inconsiderate (UK Home Office, 2003). ASB orders (ASBOs) prohibit certain acts or access to certain places, and are issued against individuals identified as causing alarm or distress to others.

Crime prevention and planning

Local authorities are expected to consider the prevention of crime and disorder as an objective in the planning process. In general, crime prevention is considered when awarding 'planning permission' – that is as part of development control. Developments judged vulnerable to crime may be required to change their design or be denied planning permission. In 2004, the Office of the Deputy Prime Minister (ODPM, 2004) published the guide 'Safer Places: The Planning System and Crime Prevention'. This document outlined clear policy statements that placed 'crime prevention at the heart of the planning process' (p. 45). 'Safer Places' drew attention to the importance of designing out crime and designing in community safety. In the UK, the police have historically played a key role in providing advice on crime prevention to both planners and designers.

The Secured by Design accreditation scheme

In 1989, the Association of Chief Police Officers (ACPO) established a crime prevention accreditation scheme named *Secured by Design* (see www.secured bydesign.com). Focusing on the design of homes and commercial buildings, the scheme promotes CPTED principles and the use of building products that conform to security standards. Secured by Design is delivered by police architectural liaison officers (ALOs) in each police force area who identify crime risks relating to a development, provide design advice and review compliance of the final design with the standard.

There is scientific evidence that Secured by Design accreditation reduces crime, antisocial behaviour and fear of crime. Properties built to the Secured by Design standard experience lower levels of crime, and their residents experience lower levels of fear of crime (Armitage, 2000, 2004, 2011; Pascoe & Topping, 1997; Teedon and Reid, 2009). Teedon and Reid (2009, cited in Armitage, 2011) conducted an evaluation of Secured By Design in Glasgow, Scotland. Their study showed that total housebreaking crime reduced by 61 per cent following the introduction of Secured By Design. This compared to a reduction of just 17 per cent in the comparison area.

The Secured by Design scheme is voluntary, and relies on developers applying for accreditation. It is up to the client to specify to the designer that their new or refurbished development should comply with the Secured by Design standard. Unfortunately, data is unavailable on the total number of developments in the UK that have achieved accreditation.

Architectural liaison service

All 43 police forces in England and Wales have traditionally employed ALOs to provide design-led crime prevention advice. The ALO is a specialist in security and crime risk management who will prepare a site-specific risk analysis and recommend appropriate measures to design out crime. However, the ALO role is usually delivered by a police officer as just one of a number of police duties. This can cause workload problems for ALOs (Wooton *et al.*, 2009).

At the outset, ALOs offered advice on large schemes, and were mainly advising local planning authorities. It is probably fair to say that it was not a very sophisticated service, and that planners were not very responsive. In the mid-1990s, new regulations, in the form of the 5/94 Government Planning Circular, resulted in crime becoming a 'material' planning consideration. This meant that crime must be taken into account when deciding whether to award planning permission to a development. As a result of this, designs for new developments began to include features and strategies to design out crime.

In 2008, the Design Against Crime Solution Centre conducted a survey of ALOs in all 43 police forces in England and Wales, which received a 78 per cent response rate. In terms of the amount of time allocated to the ALO role, the survey showed that only 14 per cent of ALOs were dedicated solely to ALO duties, and that 86 per cent of them were utilised for other, non-ALO duties. Furthermore, the amount of time dedicated to ALO activity was often relatively small, with 60 per cent of ALOs spending less than half their time on ALO activities. The survey also examined the issue of early-stage consultation on designs, asking for the approximate percentage of planning applications the ALO was consulted on before the planning application was submitted. The majority of ALOs (64 per cent) stated that they were rarely consulted at an early stage, and that early consultation took place in less than 10 per cent of cases. The survey clearly demonstrated that the ALO was not fulfilling the role of a consultant to the design process, but was more often simply commenting on finished designs. As a result, any requests for changes would be difficult to implement at such a late stage.

Redesign of GMP's ALO service

The survey revealed that not all police forces in England and Wales were taking the same approach to delivering the ALO function. One of the main departures from the norm was the service developed by Greater Manchester Police (GMP). The roots of this difference dated back to the establishment of the ALO service in GMP in the early 1990s.

In 1991, GMP appointed an architect as its first ALO. The reason for appointing an architect rather than a serving police officer – the practice in other police forces – has been lost in the mists of time, but soon became the accepted force strategy. As the ALO service expanded, the practice of appointing to ALO roles candidates from the development industry (architects, surveyors, planners, etc.) continued. This strategy was to become the foundation for the development of an ALO service unique in the UK.

In the late 1990s, GMP formed their Architectural Liaison Unit (ALU), staffed by an architect and two surveyors. By the mid-2000s (2004–2005), four ALOs were in post – all with a background in the development industry. By this stage, GMP ALOs were reviewing over 2,000 applications at the planning committee phase, from across the ten local authorities in the Greater Manchester metropolitan area.

In 2005, Manchester City Council, the biggest local authority in Greater Manchester – and so the source of most ALO work – implemented a local planning condition for Secured by Design. This stipulated that all plans had to meet the standard of the UK accreditation scheme. This action revealed a gap in GMP's ability to deliver on this Secured by Design condition, as it resulted in a large increase in workload for the ALU. At the same time, GMP did not have the resources to increase the number of ALOs. At this point, there was a 'coming together of minds' between: (a) the assistant chief constable of GMP; (b) the head of the ALU at GMP; and (c) the head of planning at Manchester City Council. A new vision for the ALU was articulated: 'To establish an innovative Architectural Liaison Unit that increases the use and effectiveness of design-led crime prevention across Greater Manchester, and becomes a focus for innovation and best practice in the Northwest' (Hodge, 2009). As well as there being more work than the current ALU could reasonably deliver, there was also a realisation of the need to do the following:

1   Influence designers much earlier in the design process
2   Formally integrate CPTED advice within the planning process
3   Generate funding to employ additional staff to cope with additional demands on the service.

This resulted in the innovation of the 'crime impact statement' (CIS). The CIS fitted with the 'impact statement' model common for considering issues in the building development industry, such as the 'environmental impact statement' and 'traffic impact statement'. The CIS was designed to enable crime prevention to be considered at a much earlier stage in a development project. Furthermore, by saving the developer money, delivery of the CIS would become something for which the developer would pay a consultation fee. This income could then support the extra staffing required by GMP to deliver a more professional architectural liaison service. So how does the CIS work?

In simple terms, the design process for the development of a building can be conceptualised as comprising three stages: (a) briefing, (b) conceptual design and (c) detailed design. These three stages may take anything from six months to several years to be completed, but generally the design process is finished prior to the application for planning permission being submitted. If the planning application is granted approval, construction can begin. Unfortunately, the majority of UK police ALOs do not get to review design proposals until a development reaches the planning application stage. In theory, ALOs should be invited by the local planning authority to comment on behalf of the police. However, this practice is far from universal. For example while one local authority might specify that the police ALO reviews plans for projects it considers to be 'major developments', another may not involve an ALO at all.

At this late stage in the process, however, any design recommendations made by an ALO will likely cause significant extra costs to the developer. These may stem from the cost of changing previously completed design proposals, the cost of delaying the construction phase or both. Consequently, an ALO process resulting in requests for 'late changes' is both unlikely to be well received by designers and developers and unlikely to be able to make significant design changes. This is a critical barrier to effective design-led crime prevention.

The goal for GMP was to integrate with the design process at an earlier stage in the development, at a point where practical crime prevention advice could be effectively integrated into the design. To enable this, GMP worked with the Design Against Crime Solution Centre to develop a new service that met the needs of developers, architects and planners – their potential clients. A service design project was undertaken by the Solution Centre that resulted in an improved means of engagement with the design development process. One finding from research undertaken on the project was that while the police used the word 'crime', planners, developers and architects tended to talk about 'security'. This insight ultimately led to the rebranding of the rather militaristic-sounding ALU as the 'Design for Security' consultancy (see Figure 8.1) and the development of communication materials that eschewed police stereotypes to project a more professional, design-oriented image (see www.designfor security.org). The ALO role was redesignated as a 'Design for Security consultant', thereby aligning with the language used in development projects.

GMP Design for Security consultants are able more often to engage with developments at the concept design stage through the mechanism of the CIS. Such early involvement lessens the risk of unexpected delays at the planning approval stage due to objections by the police. Consequently, Design for Security has been able to develop the CIS into an income-generating service, whereby developers commission the CIS. Developers pay for a timely and professional advice service, benefiting from fewer 'last-minute surprises' and costly planning delays, while GMP reinvests the income in expanding the service to meet increased workload. Experience delivering the CIS to date has shown that once the requirement to consider crime and security is understood, most architects will rise to the challenge.

The need for developments to submit a CIS with their planning application was embedded within the local planning requirements. Initially only in the Manchester City Council area, but then widening out to all ten local authorities in Greater Manchester, the CIS was included in the 'validation checklist' of documents needed to be submitted as part of an application for planning permission. The CIS merely acts as the physical endpoint to a process of consultation that takes place with the designers through the development process. The Design for Security consultant provides a critique of design proposals from a security, crime and fear of crime perspective, and acts as a 'critical friend' to the design team. As well as enabling a much more professional, customer-focused 'consultancy' approach to police crime prevention, the CIS has funded

Figure 8.1 GMP Design for Security branding. Image courtesy of Greater Manchester Police.

the expansion of the service, improved training and increased crime prevention research and evaluation opportunities.

Crime prevention services that check development designs when they are submitted for planning approval exist in certain cities (e.g. Vienna) and countries (e.g. France, the Netherlands).

Other European examples

As well as in the UK, crime prevention is being implemented across Europe using a range of different mechanisms. While some of these are nationally coordinated, practice has emerged locally in particular cities or police areas.

The Netherlands accreditation scheme

Secured by Design triggered the development of an accreditation scheme in the Netherlands called *Politiekeurmerk Veilig Wonen* (Police Label Secure Housing). This Dutch approach to incorporating crime prevention within the development of new estates was started in 1989 with a pilot project. As with the UK Secured by Design scheme, the Dutch approach is voluntary. Applicants must apply for their development to be accredited, and seek to comply with the specified standards. The label is issued to the person commissioning the building project – usually a housing association, project developer or speculative builder (Jongejan & Woldendorp, 2013).

While the English and the Dutch schemes appear similar, there are some interesting differences in terms of their background and content. The objective of the Dutch scheme is to reduce crime – principally burglary, car-related crime, theft, vandalism and nuisance – as well as to address fear of crime through environmental design, architecture and target hardening. Fire is also covered because it was recognised from the outset of the scheme's development that fire safety and security present access issues that should be considered together (Jongejan & Woldendorp, 2013).

The Dutch scheme draws on Christopher Alexander's work *A Pattern Language* (Alexander *et al.*, 1977). It focuses on urban planning and landscaping, addressing the design of the whole neighbourhood – not just a single dwelling. In 1998, the Police Label Secure Housing scheme became a Dutch standard for developing and building new estates. The Dutch scheme has reduced crime through the application of CPTED principles and by ensuring that the physical security of dwellings can withstand criminal attack (Jongejan & Woldendorp, 2013). For example a door has to be made of approved materials, conform to building regulations and pass a burglary prevention performance test. Such tests involve attack testers attempting to 'break in' using a screwdriver and a hammer. The door being tested must withstand three minutes of such assault to be approved (Davey & Jongejan, 2002).

Burglars often gain entry to houses from the rear of the property – the predominant MO of burglars in both the Netherlands and UK. Alleyways permitting access to the back of properties are not acceptable within Secured by Design due to their greater vulnerability to burglary. In contrast, in the Netherlands, alleyways are allowed due to the greater use of bicycles in that country – residents routinely park their bikes at the rear of their property. However, access to the back of a property may be controlled by installing a gate that can be locked securely. In addition, the perimeter fencing around the garden may be designed to impede access to neighbouring gardens, in case a burglar gains access to one of the neighbouring properties (Davey & Jongejan, 2002).

The Dutch label has proven extremely successful. The risk of dwellings being burgled has dropped significantly – by 95 per cent in new estates and 80 per cent in existing ones (Jongejan & Woldendorp, 2013). After it was established nationwide in 1996, police building plan advisors were trained by all the Dutch police forces. In the late 1990s, many local planning authorities in the Netherlands adopted the scheme into their planning policy guidelines. In 2004, the scheme became a Dutch building regulation. Every new estate or dwelling must now be built in accordance with the Police Label Secure Housing or an equivalent to this standard (Jongejan & Woldendorp, 2013).

In January 2005, the Police Label Secure Housing scheme entered a new phase. The previous year, the Dutch Police Force and the Ministry of the Interior decided that the Police Label Secure Housing scheme was sufficiently developed for use by the local authorities. The new approach stated that local authorities must work with building plan advisors throughout the design and management of housing and public space. The ownership of Police Label Secure Housing was transferred from the Ministry of Interior to the Dutch Centre of Crime Prevention and Safety (CCV). The CCV is responsible for the quality of the Police Label Secure Housing, and now manages the label and the list of requirements for its two application areas – new estates and the existing houses (Jongejan & Woldendorp, 2013).

Developing quality, accessibility and standards for the creation of a safe and secured environment is a challenge for the Dutch local authorities and the CCV. This is in part due to the potential fragmentation in approach, as there are more than 415 municipalities in the Netherlands responsible for planning, building and developing new and existing housing (Jongejan & Woldendorp, 2013).

The French legislation system for urban planning

The emphasis on environmental design started in France in 1995, when the *Loi d'orientation et de programmation de la sécurité* (LOPS) was enacted. This legislation made it compulsory for large construction projects to conduct an analysis of a proposed development's impact on crime. Funded by the Ministry of the Interior, the *Institut des Hautes Études sur la sécurité Intèrieure* (IHESI) was established to provide a commercial service to deliver these security assessments.

However, the institute was unable to meet the huge increase in demand. The requirement for developers to conduct a security assessment of crime and fear of crime resulted in consultancies being established to measure geographical distribution of crime, crime trends and fear of crime. In 2000, two large consultancies performed two-thirds of the total number of crime and security assessments – called DLS audits (Roché, 2002, pp. 227–28).

The safety and security network in Lower Saxony, Germany

Following a series of pilot projects, the federal state of Lower Saxony in Germany established the 'Security Partnership in Urban Development in Lower Saxony' (*Sicherheitspartnerschaft im Städtebau in Niedersachsen, SIPA*). The partnership includes police, local planning authorities, housing associations and business, and results in crime issues being raised when considering quality of life within urban planning (Schubert & Schnittger, 2005). As part of this, a quality audit scheme for secure living (QSN) has been established (http://www.sipa-niedersachsen.de). The implementation of crime prevention through urban design and planning approaches is being promoted by a police organisation in Lower Saxony – *Landeskriminalamt (LKA) Niedersachsen*. The LKA in Lower Saxony employs staff with a background in the development industry, rather than relying solely on police expertise. The wider application of the approach is being supported by research projects, including Planning Urban Security (PLuS) and Transit (Transit, 2013–2016).

Gender mainstreaming in the Viennese planning process

Despite low levels of actual crime, safety and security are considered within the planning control process in Vienna. Initiated by the City Council's 'Women's Office' (Frauenbüro), women's safety and security are covered within Vienna City Council's 'gender mainstreaming' strategy, and applied to criteria for the assessment of planning applications (Stummvoll, 2004). Plans for residential developments are reviewed by an advisory committee and, if judged to comply with the strategy, are eligible for a government subsidy. Consequently, feelings of safety are considered within most plans for residential developments in Vienna (Davey & Wootton, 2014).

A project to renovate residential areas in Szczecin (Poland)

There are also individual projects within Europe that consider crime prevention within urban design and planning. For instance a project was conducted in Szczecin to renovate courtyard areas of a residential block that attracted crime and antisocial behaviour, leading to insecurity amongst residents. Voivodeship Police Headquarters worked with local partner organisations to renovate the courtyards and establish a maintenance programme supported by residents. The incorporation of CPTED into urban design and planning is being considered (PLuS, 2009; Transit, 2013–2016).

Attempts to develop a European standard

On a European level, resources have been invested in developing a European standard in urban design and planning (Technical Report CEN TR 14383–2). However, the voluntary standard is not accepted across the whole of Europe, and has yet to be translated into a compulsory 'norm'. In 2007, it was formally accepted as a 'technical paper' intended to guide good practice (CEN, 2007; van Soomeren, 2007). To better engage different stakeholder groups, the handbook 'Planning Urban Design and Management for Crime Prevention' was published in English, French, Italian and Spanish (Politecnico di Milano, 2010). The standard does not prescribe solutions, but outlines process-based principles for the design, planning and management of urban environments. Drawing on a traditional project management approach, it provides guidance on establishing a project team, identifying problems and developing and implementing solutions. While the European standard (CEN, 2007; van Soomeren, 2007) is a potentially useful tool to support a team of stakeholders in tackling a specific, pre-existing crime problem, it seems less suited to the process of embedding crime prevention within everyday urban design and planning activities.

Development projects considering crime and/or insecurity have been implemented across Europe, albeit in a relatively ad hoc manner. Development projects disseminated in the academic literature or through websites frequently refer to CPTED theory and practice, but rarely mention the European standard. In our experience, the idea of a 'standard' or 'norm' does not appear to fit comfortably with police forces and city authorities committed to responding to local needs and conditions. Indeed, some continue to reject the approach (Grönlund *et al.*, 2016; COST TU1203).

Future policies and practices

It appears that stakeholders responsible for the design and management of the urban environment prefer to adopt an approach specific to their city, regional or national context. The opportunity to draw on theories and practices from other countries is clearly welcomed, as demonstrated by the European network on Prevention Through Urban Design and Planning (COST TU1203). However, the concept of a standardised approach applicable to all countries in Europe has not been fully embraced. As a result, pockets of good practice have been established in certain countries.

In relation to the UK, however, there are arguments that its future efficacy is being undermined by public spending cuts and changes in UK government policy to reduce so-called red tape.

Chapter 8 discussed crime prevention policies that focus on the situation confronting potential offenders in the urban context. Chapter 9 examines a crime prevention approach that focuses on the potential offender's life circumstances and development. It will introduce *Youth Design Against Crime*, which seeks to engage young people excluded from mainstream education in efforts to solve problems in their local neighbourhoods.

References

Alexander, C., Ishikawa, S. and Silverstein, M. (1977) *A Pattern Language: Towns, Buildings, Construction.* New York: Oxford University Press.

Armitage, R. (2000) 'An Evaluation of Secured by Design Housing Within West Yorkshire'. Home Office Briefing Note 7/00.

Armitage, R. (2004) Secured by Design: An Investigation of Its Jistory, Development and Future Role in Crime Reduction. Doctoral thesis, University of Huddersfield.

Armitage, R. and Monchuk, L. (2011) 'Sustaining the Crime Reduction Impact of Designing Out Crime: Re-evaluating the Secured by Design Scheme 10 years on'. *Security Journal*, Vol. 24, No. 4, pp. 320–343.

Barker, A. and Crawford, A. (2006–2009) 'Fear of Crime and Insecurity in Europe'. CrimPrev: Assessing Deviance, Crime and Prevention in Europe, Report WP4, Co-ordination Action, Framework Programme 6 (FP6). Download from: http://lodel.irevues.inist.fr/crimprev/index.php?id=330

Cozens, P.M., Saville, G. and Hillier, D. (2005) 'Crime Prevention Through Environmental Design (CPTED): A Review and Modern Bibliography'. *Property Management*, Vol. 23, No. 5, pp. 328–356.

Davey, C.L. and Jongejan, A. (2002) 'Police Label Secure Housing. Design Against Crime Case Studies'. Hippokrates 2001 Project, University of Salford.

Davey, C.L. and Wootton, A.B. (2014) The Crime Prevention Capability Maturity Model. International Perspectives of Crime Prevention 6. Contributions from the 7th Annual International Forum 2013 within the German Congress on Crime Prevention. Mönchengladbach, Germany: Forum Verlag Godesberg Gmbh. Download from: http://www.praeventionstag.de/dokumentation/download.cms?id=1922

Great Britain. (1998) 'Crime and Disorder Act 1998, Section 17'. London: HMSO.

Grönlund, B., Korthals Altes, H.J., van Sommeren, P. and Stümmvoll, G. (2014) 'Review of CEN 14383. The Death and Life of Great European Standards and Manuals. COST Action TU1203 Crime Prevention Through Urban Design and Planning'. Working Group 2. Download from: http://costtu1203.eu/downloads/cost-tu1203s-results/

Hodge, M. (2009) 'Delivering Crime Prevention: The Manchester Model'. Manchester Study Visit, delivered on 27 April as part of the EU Commission–funded project (Prevention of Fight Against Crime) on Designing Safer Communities: Crime Prevention Through Environmental Design, led by An Garda Síochána.

Home Office. (2010) *Safe and Confident Neighbourhoods Strategy: Next Steps in Neighbourhood Policing.* London: Home Office.

Jongejan, A. and Woldendorp, T. (2013) 'A Successful CPTED Approach: The Dutch "Police Label Secure Housing"'. *Built Environment*, March, Vol. 39, No. 1, pp. 31–48. Download from: http://www.veilig-ontwerp-beheer.nl/publicaties/a-successful-cpted-approach-the-dutch-2018police-label-secure-housing2019

ODPM. (2004) 'Safer Places: The Planning System and Crime Prevention'. Office of the Deputy Prime Minister. Tonbridge, UK: Thomas Telford.

Pascoe, T. (1999) 'Evaluation of Secured by Design in Public Sector Housing'. Building Research Establishment.

Pascoe, T. and Topping, P. (1997) 'Secured by Design: Assessing the Basis of the Scheme'. *International Journal of Risk, Security and Crime Prevention*, Vol. 2, No. 3, pp. 161–173.

Politecnico di Milano. (2010) 'Planning Urban Design and Management for Crime Prevention Handbook'. Politecnico di Milano, Laboratorio Qualita Urbana e Sicurezza's SAFE-POLIS Project. Download from: http://costtu1203.eu/wp-content/uploads/2014/10/Handbook-English.pdf

Roché, S. (2002) 'Towards a new Governance of Crime and Insecurity'. In A. Crawford (ed.) *France in Crime and Insecurity: The Governance of Safety in Europe*. Devon: Willan Publishing.

Schubert, H. and Schnittger, A. (2005) *Sicheres Wohnquartier Gute Nachbarschaft. Handreichung zur Förderung der Kriminalprävention im Städtebau und in der Wohnungsbewirtschaftung*. 2-Auflage. Hannover, Germany: Niedersächsischen Innenministerium.

Stummvoll, G. (2004) 'Design Against Crime in Vienna: A Feminist Approach'. *Crime Prevention and Community Safety: An International Journal*, Vol. 6, No. 4, pp. 71–82.

Teedon, P. and Reid, T. (2009) Evaluation of SBD – Glasgow Housing Association (Draft) – Architectural Liaison Officer's Conference, Nottingham, January 2009.

UK Home Office (2003) Anti-social Behaviour Act 2003. Chapter 38. London: UK Home Office. Download from: http://www.legislation.gov.uk/ukpga/2003/38/pdfs/ukpga_20030038_en.pdf

van Soomeren, P. (2007) 'Annex 15 – The European Standard for the Reduction of Crime and Fear of Crime by Urban Planning and Building Design: ENV 14383–2'. Technical Report CEN/TR 14383–2, October.

Wootton, A.B., Marselle, M., Davey, C.L., Armitage, R. and Monchuk, L. (2009) 'National Police Crime Prevention Service: Implementation Planning Research Project'. Salford, UK: DAC Solution Centre. Download from: www.npcps.org

Websites

COST Action TU1203. 'Crime Prevention Through Urban Design and Planning'. Information about the Action available from: http://www.cost.eu/domains_actions/tud/Actions/TU1203

PLuS. (2009–2012) Reports (in English, German and Polish) from the EU-funded research project 'Planning Urban Security' (PLuS) are available from: http://www.lka.polizei-nds.de/praevention/vorbeugung_themen_und_tipps/staedtebau/staedtebau-152.html

Transit. (2013–2016) 'Information About Nationally Funded Project About the Security of Residential Areas in Germany'. Transit. Download from: http://www.transit-online.info/home.html

9 The scope of Design Against Crime delivery

Since its establishment in 1999, the Design Against Crime programme has stimulated and supported practical design projects that improve safety and security through a variety of methods. Professional designers have been commissioned by the UK Design Council to use their creative research and innovation skills to tackle crime issues such as mobile phone theft and violence linked to the UK's late-night economy. The Design Council supports and publicises design exemplars of this kind as part of its remit to demonstrate the value of design in tackling complex social issues – so-called societal challenges.

As well as practising, professional designers, Design Against Crime has sought to connect with the designers of tomorrow – those in design education. From its outset, Design Against Crime has involved design students via competitive 'design challenges' focused around crime prevention. This fulfils the programme's objective to embed crime prevention within design education. In addition, children and young people with no or little experience of design have been engaged in Design Against Crime. The University of Salford and UK charity Catch22 established the *Youth Design Against Crime* (YDAC) programme to give children and young people the opportunity to apply design thinking and practice to tackling problems in their neighbourhood. Often the young people involved in YDAC projects have been identified as 'at risk of offending' by the police and education authorities. For YDAC the focus is less on the endpoint – producing an innovative design solution to a specific problem – and more on the transformative nature of the design process itself. Thus, YDAC is able to engage non-professional young designers in a process of activities that can enlighten them about issues facing others in their community, develop their thinking and problem-solving skills and dramatically improve their self-confidence and sense of self-efficacy. This is especially true for those school-age youngsters labelled as failing academically and who may be excluded from the normal school curriculum.

In order to illustrate this breadth of Design Against Crime practice, this chapter describes three projects aimed at improving safety and security through design:

- A project delivered by a team of professional designers: *reducing violence in hospital accident and emergency (A&E) departments*

- A project delivered by postgraduate design students: *preventing handbag theft in bars and cafés*
- A programme engaging young people with no formal experience of design: *Youth Design Against Crime*

Reducing violence in hospital accident and emergency departments

Since the 1990s, the Design Council has highlighted the role of design in improving public services (Burns *et al.*, 2006). As a key UK public service – arguably *the* key public service – the UK's National Health Service (NHS) has been the subject of a number of Design Council–supported projects. Despite the many benefits of a publically funded health system, it is recognised that the NHS suffers from lack of resources, difficulties retaining staff in key areas and issues with the quality of service experienced by users, such as long waiting times. In 2014, BBC Panorama reported that A&E staff were choosing to work abroad or in other hospital departments, where they perceived it to be easier to achieve a better work-life balance and quality of life (White, 2014). In recent years, the NHS has also experienced increased demand for its services from vulnerable groups due to the failure of alternative social support mechanisms. Such vulnerable groups include older people, the homeless and those dependent on drugs or alcohol. This increase in demand has precipitated problems in already busy A&E departments, often in reaction to users' unsatisfactory experience of the services provided. Recognising that designers are skilled at understanding complex systems and user experiences, the Design Council instigated a project to tackle a specific issue concerning safety and security – violence in A&E departments.

The problem of violence in A&E

The Design Council (2011) points out that violence and aggression towards frontline hospital staff have become a real problem. Each year, around 59,000 physical assaults take place in English NHS hospitals, estimated to cost the NHS at least £69 million a year in staff absence, loss of productivity and additional security. The problems are particularly acute in hospital A&E departments, which are visited by over 21 million patients each year. The combination of problems around violence and aggression and the high-pressure environment consistent with A&E results in negative experiences for both patients and staff.

The project team observed that a significant causal factor in visitors to A&E becoming frustrated was a lack of clear and effective information about the process and potential waiting times. On top of this, pain and anxiety can further reduce people's ability to cope effectively, causing some patients and family members to respond aggressively towards staff. Faced with this high-pressure environment, hospital staff found it difficult to manage visitors' frustrations effectively, further exacerbating the situation (Design Council, 2011).

The design challenge

Delivered in partnership with the UK Department of Health, the Design Council instigated a nationwide challenge that invited designers to apply their skills to help reduce violence and aggression within A&E departments. The judging panel selected a multidisciplinary design team led by PearsonLloyd to develop a range of potential solutions (https://www.designcouncil.org.uk/ projects/reducing-violence-and-aggression-ae).

Research into user behaviour and service environments is the foundation for the development of innovative solutions tailored to user needs and requirements. Desk research was conducted to better understand the issues and identify previous attempts to tackle the problem. To better understand hospital systems and visitor experience, ethnographic research was conducted by research companies at three NHS Trusts. Using interviews and observation, this research sought to understand A&E from the user's perspective. Factors that 'triggered' violent behaviour and the types of users prone to aggression were identified. It was found that aggressive behaviour was most likely amongst those who were: clinically confused, frustrated or intoxicated (Design Council, 2011, p. 3). These findings were communicated through the development of a map showing patient journeys through A&E, which highlighted where incidents of violence and aggression were most likely to occur (https://www.designcouncil. org.uk/projects/reducing-violence-and-aggression-ae).

In addition, researchers spent time with stakeholders at NHS Trusts, including managers and emergency care specialists. This enabled the researchers to understand the issues faced by frontline staff (Design Council, 2011, p. 4).

Developing and evaluating solutions

Drawing on the findings, the design team developed prototypes to test in real A&E departments. These took the form of computer models, mock-ups and initial prototypes, explains the Design Council (2011, p. 5). In the end, three solutions to help reduce anxiety and promote a positive hospital culture were developed – covering multiple aspects of the A&E service. For patients, guidance was produced in the form of a comprehensive package of information about the department, waiting times and treatment processes via on-site environmental signage, patient leaflets and digital platforms. For frontline staff, a programme of reflective practice was developed to help them manage, deal with and learn from incidents of violence and aggression. For NHS managers, clinicians, designers and healthcare planners, a package of information and guidance was produced to help them develop and deliver a better service. This was presented in the form of the *A&E toolkit* (Design Council website, 28.02.2014).

An impact evaluation of the design interventions was subsequently commissioned. This shows that the design solutions have improved patient experience, reduced non-physical hostility and aggression and provided good value for money. For instance 75 per cent of patients said the improved signage

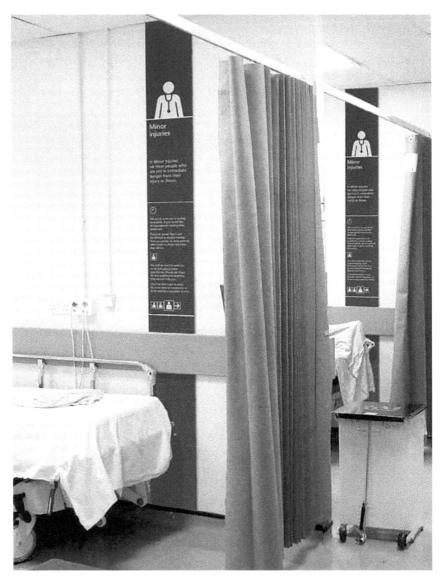

Figure 9.1 Full-height panel 'slices' within A&E (photograph by Design Council and Pearson
      Lloyd).

reduced their frustration during waiting times, and a 50 per cent reduction in
threatening body language and aggressive behaviour was recorded following
implementation of the design solutions (https://www.designcouncil.org.uk/
projects/reducing-violence-and-aggression-ae).

There are clearly potential benefits for patients, staff and taxpayers of a design intervention that successfully tackles problems. However, access to the healthcare environment often requires a range of issues to be considered, including health and safety, patient confidentiality and approval from senior management. As a result, it may be difficult to integrate such a design project within undergraduate or even postgraduate teaching and learning. There are a whole range of other contexts, though, where safety and security are important concerns, but where access for research and design purposes is potentially much easier to obtain. Situations that might be focused upon by design students include public transport hubs, public squares, city centres and the late-night economy. The next example details a design project involving students focusing on crime problems within bars and cafés.

Prevention of handbag theft in bars and cafés

A number of European universities have offered design students the opportunity to participate in crime prevention projects as part of their design education. In addition, design challenges and competitions on Design Against Crime topics have been delivered in collaboration with institutions such as the Royal Society of Arts, UK Design Council and Home Office. Design students at the Central Saint Martins College of Art & Design, part of the University of the Arts London (www.arts.ac.uk/csm/), have undertaken a number of design projects focusing on safety and security issues (Ekblom, 2012). Students were involved in a design project to prevent theft of handbags from bars and cafés. This project looked to improve on an existing anti-theft device that enables seated users to hang their handbag under the table – the 'Grippa Clip' (Ekblom *et al.*, 2012). Funded by the 'Turning the Tables on Crime Award' from the Arts and Humanities Research Council (http://www.grippaclip.com), the project involved students working in partnership with the UCL Jill Dando Institute of Crime Science. To inspire and support designers in tackling common street crimes, Central Saint Martins has developed a resource called 'In the Bag' (http://www.inthebag.org.uk/whats-in-the-bag/).

The problem of theft from handbags

While overall crime rates in England and Wales continue to drop (CSEW, 2014), theft from the person continues to be a significant problem. The number of theft-from-the-person offences rose by 8 per cent between 2002 and 2013, despite a total year-on-year decrease in other theft offences recorded by the police, including burglary, vehicle offences and bicycle theft (ONS, 2013). Researchers have pointed out that according to the 2008 British Crime Survey, people who visit cafés and bars regularly (i.e. three times a week or more) are twice as likely to be victims of theft (Ekblom *et al.*, 2012).

Theft-from-the-person offences not only are inconvenient and costly for victims but also impact on the venue owner, who may have to deal with unhappy customers (Ekblom *et al.*, 2012) as well as potential reputational damage.

For users of cafés and bars, anxiety about the safety of their belongings may detract from their enjoyment of the venue and its facilities (Ekblom *et al.*, 2012). In certain situations, it may be difficult for users to keep an eye on valuables, such as when socialising in groups, frequenting crowded venues or when under the influence of alcohol.

Limitations with current devices

Invented in 1991, the Chelsea Clip is marketed as 'the original handbag clip' by its producer, Selectamark Security Systems plc (https://www.chelseaclip.co.uk). Designed to prevent opportunist bag theft from public places, it is used to securely hang bags from bars and tables.

However, despite its proven benefits, the 'In the Bag' project researchers found that the device was considered unattractive by bar managers and inconvenient for users: 'Known problems include very low usage by customers in bars, linked to poor product semantics; being too far out of sight and hence 'out-of-mind'; and also that the objects sometimes break and can damage bags in use' (http://www.inthebag.org.uk/what-can-you-do/bag-holding-clips/chelsea-clip/).

Researching the issues

The Central Saint Martin's project aimed to develop a better alternative for enabling bar and café users to hang their handbag securely under the table. It was recognised that any design solution should prevent crime *as well as* meet the needs and requirements of the various stakeholder groups. Since crime prevention was a key objective, the design team spent some time exploring the nature and causes of theft problems in bars. Information was obtained from three sources: an analysis of police records; a review of handbag theft problems and solutions; and discussions with police crime prevention and crime reduction experts, such as architectural liaison officers (ALOs) and crime prevention design advisors (CPDAs). The research helped identify techniques and 'scripts' that enabled the offender to gain possession of a handbag and/or valuables. It also identified user and offender behaviours and environmental factors that potentially facilitate offending.

Data on patterns of handbag theft gathered by Sidebottom and Bowers (2010; cited in Ekblom *et al.*, 2012) reveal that a bag is most at risk when the owner places it over the back of their chair or on the floor at their feet. It appears that bag owners and their friends do not effectively act as 'crime preventers' because thieves are able to use stealth techniques to commit theft. Consequently, the thief's actions generally go unnoticed by the handbag owner and those they are with. Offenders will employ a range of stealth techniques to obtain a bag and/or the valuables it contains. In situations where the handbag has been placed on the floor next to the chair, the thief can wander over to the table where the bag owner is sitting and surreptitiously slide or drag the handbag towards them, often with their foot. The thief may leave the venue immediately, with the handbag perhaps hidden under a coat, or first take the bag somewhere else, such as the toilets, to empty it of any valuables. An alternative theft method is where a thief may move the bag just enough to be able to surreptitiously reach inside and remove any valuable items, such as a purse or phone. Crowded venues facilitate offenders in that they not only decrease the likelihood of the behaviour being unnoticed but also make it easier for an offender's 'excuses' to be believed if challenged: 'Sorry! My foot got caught on your bag – it's so crowded here' (Ekblom *et al.*, 2012).

Meeting all the stakeholder needs and requirements was considered a challenge. As with any design project, the design team consulted with the various stakeholders to determine their needs and requirements. This revealed the importance to bar managers and staff of factors such as cost, durability and ability to stack tables easily (Ekblom *et al.*, 2012).

The design solution – the Grippa Clip

The 'Grippa Clip' was the solution developed by the Central Saint Martins design team (Figure 9.2). Like the existing Chelsea Clip device, the Grippa Clip is a simple crime prevention mechanism that enables the user to hook

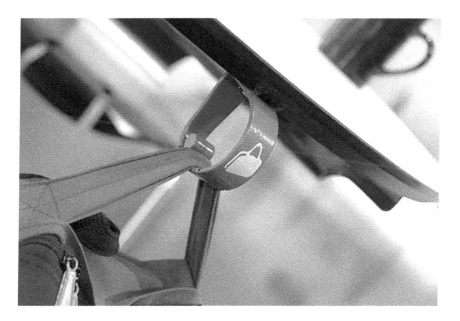

Figure 9.2 The Grippa Clip (photograph by Design Against Crime Research Centre, UAL. www.inthebag.org.uk).

their handbag over a clip, thus making stealthy removal of the bag without being noticed more difficult for the thief and therefore more risky. If detected, claimed 'innocent excuses' are unlikely to be believed. Use of such a clip also locates the bag directly within the owner's personal space (Ekblom *et al.*, 2012).

The bag is easily removed by the owner because he or she occupies a position directly in front of the Grippa Clip, and so can 'unlock' the position of the hook with one hand while the other takes the weight of the bag (Ekblom *et al.*, 2012, p. 185). It is generally better for a design solution to hinder theft without inconveniencing the user because the security measure is more likely to be used.

The Grippa Clip is made of metal, which is stronger than the plastic used for the Chelsea Clip. To encourage uptake by customers, steps were taken to engage bar management and staff in promoting use. In addition, a communication campaign was developed to raise awareness of the benefits of the clip amongst users of bars and cafés (Ekblom *et al.*, 2012).

Learning and future design projects

Interestingly, the extent to which the product was used varied between European contexts (Ekblom *et al.*, 2012). This demonstrates the context-dependency of design solutions – there are no 'one size fits all' solutions. The implementations issues and challenges presented in the development of the Grippa Clip helped generate opportunities for learning for design students, design tutors and security researchers.

To encourage others to engage in Design Against Crime, Central Saint Martins also published a range of 'takeaway briefs' that challenge designers to try designing against crime. This is ideal material for use in design education, and can be found on the project website. They have also developed a resource about theft called 'In the Bag', a website that details the causes of crime and common perpetrator techniques (MOs – modus operandi) and highlights how the design of objects or environments can reduce opportunities for crime (situational crime prevention, SCP). This resource can be viewed on the project website (http://www.inthebag.org.uk/whats-in-the-bag/).

There are real benefits to students participating in live projects. Student designers not only develop their design skills through participation in a project focusing on safety and security, but also can offer valuable insights into user experience. Higher education students are particularly vulnerable to crime. Since visiting bars and cafés is part of the student lifestyle, this may explain in part their relatively high victimisation levels in terms of theft. Other issues that might be usefully addressed by design students include burglary of student/ rented properties, mobile phone theft and violence in the late-night economy.

Youth Design Against Crime

As well as university student designers, efforts have also been made to engage school-age children and young people in using design to tackle crime. At the outset of the Design Against Crime programme, Sheffield Hallam University and the University of Salford established a partnership to deliver teaching materials to help embed crime prevention within the Design and Technology (D&T) subject area of the school curriculum. This work resulted in a number of project packs for D&T teachers to use with their students.

In 2009, the University of Salford and the UK charity Catch22 established *Youth Design Against Crime*. In 2008, Norman Lloyd, National Programme Lead for the UK charity Catch22 contacted the Design Against Crime Solution Centre at the University of Salford after having read about the Solution Centre's project in Manchester city centre – *City Centre Crime: Cooling Crime Hotspots by Design*. The project had resulted in a number of design interventions to address crime problems, and one of them – the pedestrianisation of an area experiencing problems relating to the late-night economy – was being implemented and publicised in the local press (Wootton *et al.*, 2009, 2011). At that time, Catch22's stated focus was 'helping young people out', and enabling them to overcome difficulties in their lives. Norman Lloyd asked whether young people might be engaged in the process of generating Design Against Crime solutions, using the approach developed in the City Centre Crime project.

Consequently, Catch22 collaborated with the Solution Centre to develop and trial a 10–12-week youth engagement initiative, subsequently named *Youth Design Against Crime (YDAC)*. The programme was designed specifically to meet the needs of young people excluded from mainstream education and following an 'alternative curriculum'. Such children and young people commonly have problems dealing constructively with those in positions of authority, and are often considered 'at risk of offending' (Davey *et al.*, 2012).

Establishing teams of young people

Peer group pressure can often act to promote bad behaviour in young people. Challenging the authority of teachers in a classroom setting, for example, can provide a means for young people lacking confidence to win the admiration of their peers and to develop their sense of self-esteem (Lo *et al.*, 2011). Under such circumstances, it may be tempting to separate a young person from peers considered a 'bad influence'. This 'insulating' approach is not adopted in YDAC; rather the programme seeks to build peer group relationships around constructive goals and increase participants' sense of self-efficacy. Confidence is built around constructive participation rather than defiant withdrawal.

In a YDAC project, the participating young people are divided into teams containing between five and nine members, every team being supported by a dedicated youth worker and a police mentor. Team-building activities are undertaken, including developing and collectively agreeing on a team name and identifying the group's strengths and weaknesses. The team also selects the geographic location that will form the focus of their YDAC activities, this typically being an area in their local neighbourhood. Importantly, identifying the location themselves helps foster a sense of project ownership in the teams, enabling the young people to address areas and issues of real concern to them.

Researching neighbourhood problems

Young people bring to YDAC a level of 'inside knowledge' and insight about the issues in their local areas that is often unavailable to outsiders – even their police mentors. However, while valuable, as in all good design the personal perspective is not enough. The YDAC process supports teams in moving beyond their individual experiences, guiding them in undertaking a basic design research process to understand the perspectives of others and identify the broader range of causal factors underpinning identified problems and issues. To do this, the Design Against Crime Solution Centre has developed a structured methodology to guide YDAC participants. This is communicated through the initial project workshop that kicks off each YDAC project and the YDAC Workbook provided to all participants, and is supported by the youth workers and police mentors. This YDAC process involves the teams conducting structured research to develop a 'problem profile' – a methodology that draws on the crime lifecycle model and the City Centre Crime project.

Teams of young people explore the focus area, in order to understand its importance to team members, its problems and their potential causes. In collaboration with their police mentor, the team members research crime and antisocial behaviour in the area as experienced by other users. The young people are provided with a template and questions for conducting structured interviews with different stakeholder groups.

This kicks off a process of consultation with local people that can challenge stereotypes – repositioning the young people as a potential source of solutions, rather than problems. The design research process fosters empathy, supporting teams' efforts to develop design concepts that reflect the requirements of all stakeholders, and increases opportunities for insights that can form the foundation for the creative generation of innovative solutions.

As an output of this stage, teams create a 'place-centred map' detailing changes in legitimate and illegitimate activity over time, and on which research results can be summarised and communicated.

The team uses creative ideation and brainstorming methods to develop design concepts in response to their research. These design ideas are evaluated by the team of young people in terms of their potential impact on: users; crime and antisocial behaviour; and the quality of the area. A preferred design concept is selected and further feedback sought from stakeholders regarding its strengths and weaknesses.

Showcase event to present idea

During the last few weeks of the project, the teams of young people create drawings, plan models, presentation materials and arguments to communicate the benefits of their finished design proposal to the judging panel at the YDAC Showcase Evening. At this high-profile showcase event, each team gives a short presentation to the judging panel and an audience of family, friends and invited stakeholders. Presenting at this event is both daunting and exciting, and generates a real sense of team spirit and accomplishment for the participants. The performance element of YDAC contributes to feelings of personal achievement and to a real sense of 'distance travelled' for YDAC teams (Day *et al.*, 2011, p. 62). The change in attitudes and behaviours is clearly visible to participants and observers, and is all the more significant due to the target group. YDAC participants are not used to finishing a project, or being the target for praise and further support. The young people are often shy at the beginning of the programme, and they benefit enormously from an opportunity to be heard and to influence those in positions of power.

To be able to rise up to the challenges presented by YDAC, the young people must be supported by motivated youth workers, police mentors and teachers. In our view, the research process is central to the success of YDAC. The 'creative challenge' embodied within the YDAC programme enables valuable design solutions to be developed and potentially implemented.

Delivering benefits

These examples illustrate the levels at which Design Against Crime can deliver benefits. At the professional design level, designing against crime can assist clients in solving complex problems that may be affecting their efficiency and user experience. At the student designer level, Design Against Crime can provide an opportunity for budding designers to engage with 'wicked problems' and societal challenges that affect the well-being and quality of life of large numbers of people. Finally, the design process itself can act as a creative means of engaging young people with their communities and improving self-confidence and self-efficacy, as well as providing practical, problem-solving skills of value in their future careers (Day *et al.*, 2011; Hales *et al.*, 2009; Hart,1992).

In the next chapter, we consider the impact that efforts to address safety and security are having on levels of crime across the world. The results of a crime victimisation survey show that crime is reducing, due to intervention focused on the design and security of products and environments.

References

Burns, C., Cottam, H., Vanstone, C. and Winhall, J. (2006) 'Transformational Design'. RED Paper 02. UK Design Council. Download from: http://www.designcouncil.info/mt/RED/transformationdesign/TransformationDesignFinalDraft.pdf

CSEW. (2014) 'Crime Survey for England and Wales'. January. Download from: http://www.ons.gov.uk/ons/rel/crime-stats/crime-statistics/period-ending-september-2013/stb-crime-in-england-and-wales – year-ending-sept-2013.html

Davey, C.L., Wootton, A.B. and Marselle, M. (2012) 'Engaging Young People in Design Against Crime: Design Research'. *Swedish Design Research Journal*, Vol. 1, No. 12, pp. 29–38.

Day, L., Sutton, L. and Jenkins, S. (2011) 'Children and Young People's Participation in Planning and Regeneration'. A Final Report to the Ecorys Research Programme

2010–11. Birmingham, UK: Ecorys. Download from: http://www.uk.ecorys.com/news/april2011/children-young-people-report.html

Design Council. (2011) 'Reducing Violence and Aggression in A&E – Through a Better Experience'. London: UK Design Council. Download from: http://www.designcouncil.org.uk/sites/default/files/asset/document/ReducingViolenceAndAggressionInAandE.pdf

Ekblom, P. (2012) *Design Against Crime: Crime Proofing Everyday Products.* Crime Prevention Studies, Vol. 27. London: Lynne Rienner.

Ekblom, P., Bowers, K., Gammon, L., Sidebottom, A., Thomas, C. Thorpe, A. and Wilcocks, M. (2012) 'Reducing Handbag Theft'. In P. Ekblom (ed.) *Design Against Crime: Crime Proofing Everyday Products.* Crime Prevention Studies, Vol. 27. London: Lynne Rienner. Chapter 9, pp. 167–200.

Hales, J., Nevill, C., Pudney, S. and Tipping, S. (2009) 'Longitudinal Analysis of the Offending, Crime and Justices Survey, 2003–06. Key Implications'. Research Report 19, Home Office, November 2009. ISBN 978–1–84987–100–6. Download from: http://webarchive.nationalarchives.gov.uk/20110218135832/rds.homeoffice.gov.uk/rds/pdfs09/horr19c.pdf

Hart, R.A. (1992) *Children's Participation: From Tokenism to Citizenship.* Florence, Italy: UNICEF.

Lo, T.W., Cheng, C.H.K., Wong, D.S.W., Rochelle, T.L. and Kwok, S.I. (2011) 'Self-Esteem, Self-Efficacy and Deviant Behaviour of Young People in Hong Kong'. *Advances in Applied Sociology*, Vol. 1, No. 1, pp. 48–55.

ONS. (2013) 'Statistical Bulletin: Crime in England and Wales'. Year Ending June 2013 National Statistics Part of Crime Statistics, period ending June 2013 Release, London: Office of National Statistics. Download from: http://www.ons.gov.uk/ons/rel/crime-stats/crime-statistics/period-ending-june-2013/stb-crime-in-england-and-wales – year-ending-june-2013.html#tab-Summary

Sidebottom, A. and Bowers, K. (2010) 'Bag Theft in Bars. An Analysis of Relative Risk, Perceived Risk and *Modus Operandi*'. *Security Journal*, Vol. 23, No. 3, pp. 206–224.

White, V. (2014) 'A&E Doctors Heading to Australia "for a Better Life"'. BBC Panorama, 17 March. Download from: http://www.bbc.com/news/uk-26559034?print=true

Wootton, A.B., Davey, C.L. and Marselle, M. (2011) 'Design Against Crime: A Catalyst for Change Amongst Young People'. 9th European Academy of Design Conference 'The Endless End', Porto, Portugal, 4–7 May. Download from: http://endlessend.up.pt/site/wp-content/uploads/2011/05/EAD9-Conference-Proceedings_r.pdf

Wootton, A.B., Marselle, M. and Davey, C.L. (2009) 'City Centre Crime: Design Thinking for Safer City Centres'. 8th European Academy of Design Conference, The Robert Gordon University, Aberdeen, Scotland, 1–3 April. Download from: http://usir.salford.ac.uk/12531/

Websites

Central Saint Martins website, 'Design Against Crime Research Centre, "In the Bag" Project'. Download from: http://www.inthebag.org.uk/what-can-you-do/bag-holding-clips/chelsea-clip/

Design Council website (28.02.2014) 'Report on Reducing Violence and Aggression in Accident and Emergency Departments, in Partnership with Department of Health'. Download from: https://www.designcouncil.org.uk/projects/reducing-violence-and-aggression-ae

Part IV

Applications and futures

10 Crime victimisation

A global perspective

Our everyday action reflects the tacit understanding that our behaviour and good design can impact on crime. Homeowners install alarms, bike riders routinely lock their bicycles to secure bike stands and car owners opt for safe locations to park their vehicles. The reader may be surprised to learn the extent to which design and user behaviour affect crime levels worldwide. Drawing on the findings of scientific studies, this chapter reviews the contribution housing and vehicle design makes to reducing crime levels worldwide. The findings lend further support to the proposition that opportunity is a critical 'causal factor', tempting potential offenders to offend. Furthermore, such opportunities may introduce young people to offending behaviour, with the risk of inducing some into a life of crime. One important research tool is the International Crime Victimisation Survey (ICVS). More than 70 countries have participated at least once over the years, making this an invaluable tool for guiding and evaluating crime prevention policy and practice. Unfortunately, in these years of austerity, the funding and management of such large-scale scientific studies are problematic. Without a strong scientific evidence base, there is a danger that changing political priorities can undermine efforts to effectively address crime issues. Policymakers must not allow the value of effective, design-led crime prevention in reducing victimisation – along with all the negative consequences for the individual and society victimisation brings – to be subsumed by short-term political agendas.

Crime, morality and poverty

Crime and security are highly emotive subjects, embracing beliefs about morality, politics and economics. As noted in Chapter 7, the political left has traditionally blamed offending behaviour on societal causes, such as poverty and social deprivation, preferring to focus on improving social conditions for citizens and offender rehabilitation rather than on punishment. This role of crime and disorder in political discourse and government policy is explored by academics and practitioners (Roché, 2002; Waiton, 2006). In relation to the UK, Waiton points out that:

> The politicisation of crime can be dated back to the 1970s, with the 1970 Conservative government being the first to identify as the party of law and

order. As crime developed as a political issue through the 1970s, however, it was fiercely contested. When Conservatives shouted 'law and order', the left would reject the idea that crime was increasing or was a social problem in and of itself, pointing instead to the social problems thought to underlie it.

(Waiton, 2006, p. 2)

The role of poverty in offending behaviour is worthy of further discussion, since the conclusions impact on policies at national and international levels. Scientific research shows that, under some circumstances, economic hardship causes an increase in crime. For example a study of crime within the German federal state of Bavaria between 1835 and 1861 indicated a strong link between the price of bread and number of people arrested for theft of bread and vagrancy (Bonger, 1905, cited by van Dijk, 2012). However, in the twenty-first century, national prosperity does not appear to result in less crime within the nation state. Criminology professor Jan van Dijk makes the point that the data on crime victimisation does not reveal a straightforward correlation between affluence and crime (van Dijk *et al.*, 2012, p. 2). Some wealthier European countries suffer from comparatively high crime rates – for instance Switzerland and Denmark. Meanwhile some less affluent countries experience fairly low crime rates, such as Portugal, Hungary and Spain (van Dijk *et al.*, 2007, p. 43). In fact, there is some evidence that crime levels increase with growing prosperity. Between the 1960s and mid-1990s, when crime levels consistently increased, gross domestic product (GDP) – commonly used as an indicator of national wealth – increased significantly. In addition, most countries introduced welfare states to provide a safety net for poorer sections of society. In their book *The International Crime Drop*, van Dijk *et al.* suggest that 'Problems of crime and juvenile delinquency manifested themselves not as a product of the economic crisis but as by-products of the *wirtschaftwunder* [economic miracle]' (van Dijk *et al.*, 2012, p. 3). The outbreak in criminal activity that started in the 1960s and lasted until the mid-1990s became known as the 'crime epidemic'. Policymakers appeared powerless to prevent further increases. Van Dijk (2012) suggests that for criminologists at the time, it was hard to envisage a decline in crime levels. This sense of powerlessness stemmed in part from the way in which offending behaviour was understood. The crime problem was attributed to 'moral decline' and the 'breakdown of society' – a line of reasoning that offered little in the way of practical solutions.

Opportunity theory offers alternative explanation

In 1979, Cohen and Felson published an article in the *American Sociological Review* theorising that the crime boom was due to an increase in criminal opportunities offered by an increasingly consumerist society. The authors attributed opportunities for crime to social and technological developments, such as the widespread use of consumer products attractive to thieves, and houses left unoccupied during the day as more women chose to work outside of the home.

In 1998, Marcus Felson and Ronald V. Clarke published their seminal work 'Opportunity Makes the Thief'. The authors argued that opportunities play a role in causing all crime, not just common property crime. For example studies of bars and pubs show how design and management impact on levels of violence. Credit card and other frauds can be prevented by better design and security. Even sexual offences and drug dealing may be prevented by reducing opportunities, or providing alternatives.

Felson and Clarke (1998) used a study of suicide levels to illustrate the impact of opportunity on behaviour that is not normally considered 'opportunistic'. Suicide is perceived to be a deeply motivated act, committed only by people who are disturbed and depressed over a long period of time. Nevertheless, Felson and Clarke were able to show that opportunity plays an important role in determining even this desperate act. In 1958, 5,298 people committed suicide in England and Wales, with around a half using domestic gas to kill themselves – usually via gas ovens. At that time, the domestic gas was manufactured from coal, and was lethal due to its high carbon monoxide content. In 1968, manufactured 'town gas' began to be replaced by natural gas, which is almost entirely free of carbon monoxide. By the mid-1970s, natural gas was being used throughout England and Wales. Between 1968 and 1975, the total number of suicides dropped from 5,298 to 3,693, with the final figure including less than 1 per cent of suicides committed using domestic gas. In other words, the suicide rate was reduced when an easily available opportunity to commit suicide – domestic 'town gas' – was removed. This reduction occurred despite the period being one of significant economic change and uncertainty, which might be predicted to increase suicidal feelings in the population. Despite what one might expect, people who felt suicidal did not simply turn to alternative methods. In this way, even suicide can be considered an opportunist act, and so prevented using a situational approach.

There were of course criticisms from academics wedded to other approaches, such as cultural criminology. In 2010, an excellent rebuttal to critics of situational crime prevention (SCP) was provided by the criminology professor Graham Farrell. His article explores the many ways in which SCP theory can be used to tackle crime, including those offences strongly motivated by so-called expressive factors, such as fun, excitement, pleasure and perceived status amongst peers (Farrell, 2010). Further support for the SCP approach has come from data on changing crime levels and patterns.

Opportunity theory explains reduction in crime level

From the mid-1990s onward, despite some exceptions, crime rates began to decline across the industrialised world. We know that urban areas suffer from higher levels of crime compared to non-urban areas (van Dijk, 2012/3), so this downward trend is remarkable considering that the number of people living in urban areas has increased during this same period. As the United Nations Population Fund (UNFPA) points out, 'The world is undergoing the largest wave of urban growth in history. In 2008, for the first time in history, more than half of the world's population will be living in towns and cities' (UNFPA, 2014). Various attempts have been made to explain this phenomenon. Some researchers and practitioners attribute the drop in crime in the United States to changes in national policies and practices. These include a wide range of measures, from the introduction of zero tolerance policing in New York, through changes to the US policy on abortion, to even capital punishment (Farrell, 2013). The difficulty with these US-centric explanations, however, is that the decline in crime rates has been experienced across the industrialised world. The so-called crime drop cannot therefore be attributed to a single national policy or practice, but must relate to factors capable of operating across country contexts.

In 2007, the authors of the ICVS proposed an explanation that linked the crime drop to improved security design. Van Dijk *et al.* (2007) credit better car security design with reducing theft of and from vehicles worldwide. They argue that better security limits opportunistic crime, acts to confine vehicle crime to a more motivated and skilled minority, and prevents a wider group of potential offenders from 'dabbling' in crime:

> In recent years overall rates of car theft have gone down almost everywhere. Trend data on 13 countries show that this downward trend is fully caused by a drop in the less professional forms such as theft for joyriding. Anti-theft devices limiting easy opportunities for amateur thieves seem to be the most likely explanation for this universal drop.
>
> (van Dijk *et al.*, 2007, p. 13)

Similarly, reductions in burglary worldwide are attributed to better security of residential dwellings vulnerable to crime (van Dijk *et al.*, 2007). 'Improved security among sufficiently large proportions of vulnerable households may have dissuaded potential burglars from committing burglaries by increasing efforts and risks' (van Dijk *et al.*, 2007, p. 68). The role of opportunity, design and security in generating crime, or preventing its occurrence, is beginning to be communicated more widely. In 2013, *The Economist* published an article entitled 'The Curious Case of the Fall in Crime', pointing out that the biggest single factor behind the drop in crime 'is simply that security measures have improved' (The Economist, p. 9). *The Economist* article pointed out that the inclusion of vehicle immobiliser technology in car security design has 'killed joyriding' and better design and security made bank robberies far too risky. Hopefully, wider reporting of the value of design-led crime prevention will convince policymakers and decision-makers of the advantage of taking a design approach to security.

In 2013, Farrell published a paper testing the competing theories put forward to explain the drop in crime. Each theory claims to explain changing levels of offending, attributing this to a range of factors, including demographic change, capital punishment, lead in petrol, abortion policy, policing strategy and improved security. The security hypothesis, based on opportunity theory, is the only one to stand up to close scrutiny. The security hypothesis suggests that more and better security drove the crime drop, and this is supported by data from the UK, Australia and the United States. The hypothesis can account for changes in the levels of different crime types. It offers a credible explanation as to why, while other crimes have fallen, there have been increases in mobile phone theft and Internet-related crimes (Farrell, 2013).

Crime in different countries

As mentioned earlier, crime levels vary across different countries. The level and type of crime experienced by a nation depend upon the opportunities offered by the particular contexts within it. More densely populated countries tend to suffer more crime overall, although there are a few exceptions. For example the Republic of Ireland is high in crime, but not densely populated. Notwithstanding such exceptions, higher density can generally be linked to higher crime rates, resulting in cities suffering around 4 per cent more crime compared to other areas (van Dijk *et al.*, 2007).

Variations in product ownership and use can impact on both level and type of crime. For example the Netherlands suffers from high levels of bike theft simply because bicycles are a common choice of transport. Similarly, countries with relatively high levels of alcohol consumption *per capita* tend to suffer more from violent crime (van Dijk *et al.*, 2007). Alcohol consumption increases the likelihood of conflict and violence in the domestic and public realm, and is also associated with problems of antisocial behaviour in public spaces (Manchin *et al.*, 2005).

Countries are not helpless in the face of such problems, however. Through better design and security, countries like the UK and the Netherlands have successfully reduced burglary from the high levels experienced in the 1990s. Indeed, the UK and Netherlands are at the forefront of efforts to prevent crime, introducing accreditation schemes for buildings and environments, such as Secured by Design in the UK and Police Label Secure Housing in the Netherlands. This is supported by the fact that British and Dutch citizens are willing to use security measures such as security alarms on houses.

In contrast, Denmark suffered a 33 per cent increase in burglary between 2005 and 2010. This is attributed to a reluctance amongst policymakers and citizens to introduce security measures for residential buildings. One result of the increased burglary rate – and its implications for quality of life – is that Danish attitudes appear to be changing. By 2010, the percentage of Danish citizens worried about being burgled had risen to twice that of citizens elsewhere in Western Europe (van Dijk, 2012/3). In 2012, the Danish Crime Prevention Council was commissioned to explore the potential for embedding crime prevention within design and planning in Denmark. A group of architects and planners visited both Manchester (UK) and Amsterdam (NL) to review

Table 10.1 Victimisation by burglary; one-year victimisation rates for 2009–2010 (percentages) and results of available previous surveys (1989–2005).

	1989	1992	1996	2000	2005	2010
Canada	3.0	3.4	3.4	2.3	3.0	1.3
Denmark	–	–	–	3.1	2.7	3.6
Estonia	–	6.0	4.2	3.7	2.5	3.0
Georgia	–	2.5	3.6	2.6	7.1	0.5
Germany	1.3	–	–	–	0.9	1.2
Netherlands	2.4	2.0	2.6	1.9	1.3	0.8
Sweden	–	1.4	1.3	1.7	0.7	1.0
Switzerland	1.0	–	1.3	1.1	1.6	1.9
England and Wales	2.1	–	2.8	2.7	3.3	1.5

Source: ICVS 1989–2010; see http://wp.unil.ch/icvs/category/uncategorized.

design-led crime prevention processes and practices in these cities. Over the longer term, Denmark may therefore be able to reduce its burglary problem.

Some countries are reaping the benefits of crime prevention practices instigated several decades ago. In Germany, for example, steering wheel locks were made compulsory in the 1980s. This policy helped reduce vehicle crime in a country with high levels of car ownership (Mayhew, 1992). Van Dijk (2012) credits this early German policy with producing wider, longer-term benefits. Joyriding is considered to be a 'debut crime', as it can introduce young people to further, more serious offending behaviour. Consequently, the German policy to tackle vehicle crime will have helped reduce other crimes as well, by closing this route into habitual offending.

The instance of a targeted crime prevention measure acting to slow or cease other categories of crime is what is termed a 'diffusion of benefits'. Researchers have tested whether crime prevention efforts simply result in what is termed 'displacement' – the idea that crime prevented in a particular location or against a particular target simply 'moves around the corner'. Evidence suggests that while some crime may be displaced, it is not displaced in its entirety, so the overall benefit of prevention remains. This is because many offenders are easily deflected from committing offending behaviour – much of which, as already discussed, is opportunistic. Offenders are not committed to offending at whatever cost. Another barrier to displacement relates to the offenders' capabilities. Offenders develop distinct knowledge and skills relating to the types of crimes they customarily commit, which is an obstacle to them easily changing their targets, locations or MOs. Indeed, as the German example highlights, crime prevention measures can spread improvements beyond the area targeted by a security intervention. One reason put forward for why this may occur is that offenders overestimate the reach and effectiveness of the crime prevention measures of which they become aware (Weisburd & Green, 1995; Weisburd et al., 2005).

Crime waves and technological development

While there may have been an overall fall in crime, some specific types of crimes are actually on the increase. For example street robbery has emerged as an increasing problem since the 1990s due to the development and growth in the use of mobile phones (Harrington & Mayhew, 2001).

Crime wave linked to mobile phones

According to the Crime Survey for England and Wales, mobile phone theft rose 663 per cent from 1993 to its peak in 2003/4, from 93,158 to 617,721 incidents per year. Although it has dropped slightly since this time, it still stood at 524,541 incidents in 2011/12 – some 563 per cent higher than in 1993. Research shows that mobile phones were involved in 46 per cent of all robberies in 2011/12, compared to just 8 per cent in 1998. Mobile phone theft is of particular concern to governments and citizens because victims are often young. Thirty-seven per cent of victims of mobile phone theft are between 14 and 24 years of age, with a further 4 per cent below the age of 13 years. Young women aged 18 to 24 were at the highest risk of mobile phone theft victimisation. Offenders were also young, with 58 per cent of offences being carried out by those aged 16 to 24 years.

Source: Office for National Statistics (2013).

The development of the Internet, online and mobile communications technologies and e-commerce has generated new opportunities for some types of crime, such as corruption, fraud and the illegal copying of copyrighted materials. The Internet has also enabled individuals to more easily access illicit or unlawful material, and co-offenders to contact and share information between each other. This has provided opportunities for organised crime and those involved in illegal activities, such as the trafficking of human beings, money laundering and illegal drugs. As the towns and cities we live in change and grow, and as new products, services and technologies are developed, opportunities for undesirable and criminal behaviour emerge and evolve. To effectively tackle such problems, there is a need for accurate data on crime levels and offending behaviour.

Measuring crime levels

Much information about crime comes from the ICVS. Initiated in 1987, this survey is conducted on households in different countries every four years. Participants in the ICVS are asked about their experiences of ten prevalent crimes over the past 12 months – crimes broadly defined as vehicle-related, burglary, theft of personal property and contact crime (robbery, sexual offences, and assault and threat). The results from the survey sample are used to determine the level of crime in the country, and to identify crime trends and patterns through comparison with previous surveys. The data obtained can be used to draw comparisons between countries, in terms of crime levels and trends. Information is also collected about subjective issues, such as satisfaction with police services (van Dijk *et al.*, 2007).

The ICVS surveys have traditionally been conducted by telephone, but more recently online methodologies have been piloted. The number of households surveyed is relatively small – only 2,000 in each country. However, the surveys are a valuable method for drawing comparisons between countries, which is not possible with police data. Unfortunately, funding problems have delayed the administration of the survey and recent reports include survey findings from only 12 countries. This seems unfortunate since the ICVS offers independent data on crime levels that can be compared over time and between national contexts. Such data is invaluable to guiding and evaluating crime and security policies and practices at national, European and international levels.

Information about offending behaviour is found from self-report surveys, where individuals are asked about their participation in criminal activities. Scientific studies demonstrate the accuracy of self-reported data, which strongly correlates with recorded instances of criminal activity. Such data identifies patterns and trends in offending behaviour, and is valuable in understanding the causes of crime (Farrington, n.d.).

The final chapter of the book, Chapter 12, will examine the future role of design in safety and security practice, policy and research –in terms of both design professionals and design students.

References

Bonger, W.A. (1905) 'Criminality and Economic Conditions', published in English by the Political Economy Club, 1916, Vancouver, BC, Canada. Cited in van Dijk, J. (2012) 'Closing the Doors'. Stockholm Prizewinners Lecture 2012. Download from: http://www.criminologysymposium.com/download/18.4dfe0028139b9a0cf4080001575/TUE13,+van+Dijk+Jan.pdf

Cohen, L.E. and Felson, M. (1979) 'Social Change and Crime Rate Trends: A Routine Activity Approach'. *American Sociological Review*, Vol. 44, pp. 588–605.

The Economist. (2013) 'The Curious Case of the Fall in Crime'. *Leaders, The Economist*, 20 July. Download from: http://www.economist.com/news/leaders/21582004-crime-plunging-rich-world-keep-it-down-governments-should-focus-prevention-not

Farrell, G. (2010) 'Situational Crime Prevention and Its Discontents: Rational Choice and Harm Reduction Versus "Cultural Criminology" '. *Social Policy and Administration*, Vol. 44, No. 1, pp. 40–66.

Farrell, G. (2013) 'Five Tests for a Theory of the Crime Drop'. Paper presented at International Symposium on Environmental Criminology and Crime Analysis (ECCA), Philadelphia, PA.

Farrington, D.P. (n.d.) 'What Has Been Learned from Self-Reports About Criminal Careers and the Causes of Offending'. Report for the Home Office.

Felson, M. and Clarke, R.V. (1998) 'Opportunity Makes the Thief: Practical Theory for Crime Prevention'. Police Research Paper 98. London: Home Office.

Harrington, V. and Mayhew, P. (2001) 'Mobile Phone Theft: Home Office Research Study'. Home Office Development and Practice Report No. 17. London: Home Office. Download from: http://www.publicsafety.gc.ca/cnt/rsrcs/lbrr/ctlg/shwttls-eng.aspx?d=PS&i=2789439

Manchin, R., van Dijk, J., van Kesteren, J., Nevala, S. and Hideg, G. (2005) 'The Burden of Crime in the EU. Research Report: A Comparative Analysis of the European Crime and Safety Survey (EU ICS) 2005'. Download from: http://vorige.nrc.nl/redactie/binnenland/Misdaad.pdf

Mayhew, P. (1992) 'Steering Column Locks and Car Theft'. In R.V. Clarke (ed.) *Situational Crime Prevention: Successful Case Studies*. Albany, NY: Harrow and Heston, pp. 52–65.

Office for National Statistics. (2013) 'Chapter 2: Mobile Phone Theft'. Crime Statistics, Focus on Property Crime, 2011/12, London: ONS. Download from: http://www.ons.gov.uk/ons/dcp171776_309772.pdf

Roché, S. (2002) 'Towards a New Governance of Crime and Insecurity'. In A. Crawford (ed.) *France in Crime and Insecurity: The Governance of Safety in Europe*. Devon: Willan Publishing.

UNFPA, 'Urbanization: A Majority in Cities'. The United Nations Population Fund. Download from: https://www.unfpa.org/pds/urbanization.htm (accessed 10.03.2014).

van Dijk, J. (2012) Closing the Doors. Highlights of the Crime Victimis Survey, 1987–2012. Tilburg, The Netherlands, 7 December, 2012. Download from: https://pure.uvt.nl/ws/files/1519203/120665_afsch_rede_van_Dijk_final.pdf

van Dijk, J. (2012/3) 'The International Crime Victims Survey, Latest Results and Prospects, in "Criminology in Europe" '. *Newsletter of the European Society of Criminology*, 2012, Vol. 11, No. 3, pp. 24–25. Download from: http://wp.unil.ch/icvs/2013/04/445/

van Dijk, J., Tseloni, A. and Farrell, G. (2012) 'Introduction'. In J. van Dijk, A. Tseloni and G. Farrell (eds.) *The International Crime Drop: New Directions in Research*. Crime Prevention and Security Management. Houndsmill, Basingstoke: Palgrave Macmillan. pp. 1–8.

van Dijk, J., van Kesteren, J. and Smit, P. (2007) 'Criminal Victimisation in International Perspective: Key Findings from the 2004–2005 ICVS and EU ICS'. The Hague, Netherlands: WODC.

Waiton, S. (2006) 'Anti-social Behaviour: The Construction of a Crime'. *Spiked*, 19 January 2006. Available at: http://www.spiked-online.com/newsite/article/5#.V_y27hSAS9o

Weisburd, D. and Green, L. (Mazerolle) (1995) 'Measuring Immediate Spatial Displacement: Methodological Issues and Problems'. In J. E. Eck and D. Weisburd (eds.) *Crime and Place*. Crime Prevention Studies, Vol. 4. Monsey, NY: Willow Tree Press. pp. 349–361.

Weisburd, D., Wyckoff, L.A., Ready, J. Eck, J.E. Hinkle, J. and Gajewski, F. (2005) 'Does Crime Just Move Around the Corner? A Study of Displacement and Diffusion in Jersey City, NJ'. U.S. Department of Justice. Download from: https://www.ncjrs.gov/pdffiles1/nij/grants/211679.pdf

11 The future

In this final chapter, we summarise some of the main arguments of the book, considering the extent to which crime prevention can be embedded in design. We also look to the future, noting the implications for security of developments in technologies, cuts in public spending and societal changes. We believe that designers can play an important role in creating a safer society and urge governments to promote responsible innovation.

Safer designs

We contend that crime prevention and a more sophisticated understanding of safety must be embedded within the notion of 'professional design practice'. Most professionals must follow codes of conduct that lay down rigorous ethical and moral obligations. An example of this is the Hippocratic oath, traditionally sworn by medical doctors. For designers, 'professionalism' is increasingly related to a consideration of wider ethical, environmental and social issues that impact the society in which they practise. We suggest that victimisation due to crime is just such an issue. From victimisation studies and numerous practical examples, the value of design in reducing the likelihood of users becoming victims of crime is evident. Furthermore, careful design is a means to ensure that places, services and products retain their value for users by, for instance, being resistant to damage or easily repaired.

In Europe, the main focus to date has been on crime and disorder issues within urban design, with designers playing an important role in tackling crime and feelings of insecurity. This is generally a collaborative effort, with designers working together with planners, managers and police to anticipate potential problems and prevent them occurring in the first place. Steps are being taken to go beyond ad hoc projects that address already existing problems, to develop more strategic or systematic approaches that prevent crimes from occurring in the first place (Davey & Wootton, 2014a). We have argued that consideration of crime issues at an early stage in the design development process can improve user safety, without increasing fear of crime, and can contribute to a better quality of life.

Most people probably agree that crime prevention should be integrated into design and planning in high-crime contexts. In our view, vulnerability to crime should be considered *routinely* – in all contexts. Otherwise, opportunities for crime may be inadvertently built in. Even safe environments can become crime hotspots due to facilities and design features that act as magnets for criminals and support offending behaviour. We are aware of residential neigh-bourhoods becoming targets for domestic burglaries when a footpath is created (Davey *et al.*, 2009), office buildings being subject to commercial burglaries because media and computing equipment is located on the ground floor and retail shops suffering high levels of shoplifting because valuable products are on display near an entrance or exit. Situations vulnerable to crime gener-ate insecurity for a range of groups of people – including users, neighbours, office staff and security staff. They also result in police and local authorities being called upon to respond to problems of crime and insecurity, and perhaps prevent them from happening again. From the government's point of view, it therefore makes sense to ensure that organisations integrate crime prevention into the design of their buildings, products and services.

Expanding the role of design

Safety and security principles are being applied to a range of designs and contexts, including residential dwellings, commercial properties, schools and transport hubs, ATMs, post offices and banks. This can increase the safety of services particularly prone to problems of crime and antisocial behaviour problems. We firmly believe that designers can play a much wider role in shaping our cities and improving the urban experience. This goes beyond merely the physical fabric of the city, and includes the systems, services and processes that are involved in its management and use. We have seen that designers can work with police forces to improve the services they deliver to developers, and with planners to improve the way in which planning con-trol decisions are taken (Davey & Wootton, 2015; Wootton & Davey, 2015). Indeed, the role of design in supporting public sector improvement is increas-ingly recognised. The global design company IDEO is applying its private sector knowledge, connections and experience to government and non-profit projects (http://www.ideo.com/expertise/public-sector/). The UK Design Council has established a portfolio of projects to improve the public ser-vices, and is a strong advocate for design to contribute to the public sector: 'how design approaches can be used to tackle some of our most urgent chal-lenges, such as the integration of health and social care services and efficiency improvement within local government' (Finnegan, 2016). In addition, vari-ous European networks, such as 'Design for Europe', specifically highlight the role of design in helping to generate innovative and creative solutions to some of the challenges facing the public sector (http://designforeurope.eu/public-sector).

From city vision to urban experience

Designers can work with local authorities to develop a vision for cities in the future that are truly 'livable' by providing insight into human feelings, emotions and experience. This is an aspect of urban existence that has been somewhat neglected. Over the last two decades, city leaders in the UK have focused on the economic success of cities. Local authorities have invested in improving retail areas and in supporting the development of the late-night economy. Such facilities are often developed as a part of a wider vision to create vibrant cities that remain active over a 24-hour period, incorporating elements from what is often portrayed as a 'continental' model of the metropolis – cafés, opportunities to eat and drink outside and public squares where formal and informal events and activities are routinely staged. However, too often the development of bars and clubs has fuelled a binge drinking culture that generates crime and disorder problems, including within locations where students live and socialise (Home Office, 2014). This can impact negatively on the quality of urban living for some groups, such as residents living near to drinking venues, families with young children and older citizens.

In cities across continental Europe, well-designed public spaces are viewed as a means to facilitate interaction between citizens and allow users to simply experience the urban environment, without necessarily purchasing food or drink. Public squares and spaces in cities such as Copenhagen, Stockholm, Prague and Barcelona very much contribute to the quality of the urban environment (Gehl, 2010; http://gehlarchitects.com/work/cases/).

The development and maintenance of quality urban space can be difficult in underused areas, and within deprived communities. These types of locations are often unattractive to the private sector, and the public sector may be unwilling or unable to provide the necessary investment to ensure the location remains attractive to legitimate users. Nevertheless, there are examples where public space has been developed, continues to be well maintained and is being used regularly by a whole range of people, including those on the margins of society – the homeless, poor, unemployed and buskers. In addition, problems such as drug dealing, vandalism and antisocial behaviour are kept under control in some way. This means that problems are significantly reduced in frequency or seriousness, impact minimally on other user groups and/or are dealt with cost-effectively. In Barcelona, for instance, a public library and surrounding gardens have been renovated to improve education and quality of life in a deprived district (Stummvoll *et al.*, 2014).

In Anna Minton's report 'The Privatisation of Public Space' (2006), she documents the ways in which public space is gradually being privatised. The privatisation of public spaces may limit the development of areas within the city centre and in shopping malls.

Smart cities: data versus design

Cities around the globe are striving to become 'smart cities'. This means getting smarter, joining up services and collecting data in order to improve city life for citizens and save money for local authorities. Technology firms promise to help streamline traffic management, rubbish collections and street lights.

Data is seen as key to making cities smarter, and a network of sensors aims to connect everything to the network and create new services for citizens. As part of this, technology firms are designing more community-developed apps that use the power of the crowd – for instance to offer real-time maps of city traffic flow (Wakefield, 2013).

The Scottish city of Glasgow is striving to be the 'first smart city in the world'. The *Future Cities* project is using Information and Communications Technology (ICT) to address a range of issues in Glasgow, some of which are related to crime and safety. For instance Glasgow is using 'big data' to forecast outbreaks of crime, installing street lights that measure footfall and aim to stop brawls and mapping 400 patches of empty land with a view to providing cyclists with an app to help inform its decisions about where to create bike lanes (http://futurecity.glasgow.gov.uk/index.aspx?articleid=10213).

However, there have been doubts raised about the validity of technological approaches to understanding and addressing problems, especially 'big data'. We do not believe 'big data' to be the solution to problems, and note increasing scepticism over its much trumpeted value (The Economist, 2014; Harford, 2014).

The main shortcoming with the smart cities approach is its focus on technology solutions rather than human-centred ones. As others have pointed out, the 'big data' approach relies on detecting patterns in large data sets, and prioritises correlation over causation (The Economist, 2014). But when tackling a 'wicked problem' like crime in an environment populated by socially and culturally complex beings like humans, understanding causation is critical if human well-being is a priority. But big data is blind, and so cannot fully consider the 'urban experience' from the point of view of the resident, user or citizen. We suggest that the smart cities approach has new managerialist roots. Urban problems are perceived as problems of management rather than issues of human experience, and so do not get to the heart of what city living represents for the residents or neighbourhoods. Nor does it capture the quality of life aspects associated with hanging around, moving about and participating in activities – the vibrancy, spontaneity, opportunities for connection to others, the aliveness, the 'delight' and 'buzz' of the city centre experience.

The connected city – for real!

City living offers residents the opportunity to live in a vibrant environment, in proximity to urban cultural and social amenities. Informal contact with neighbours can not only improve quality of life but also help to break down cultural barriers to sharing problems and providing mutual support. With more women returning to work, residential buildings housing families may be fairly quiet during the day. This may contribute to older people, the unemployed, parents looking after babies and preschool children full-time feeling lonely and socially isolated. In addition, the development and maintenance of social networks close to the home environment are increasingly difficult, as people travel further afield for schools and jobs, move home in order to find work, work long hours, use childcare services, separate or divorce or live some distance from family and loved ones. This reduces opportunities for social contact between neighbours and, without active intervention, may impact negatively on the vibrancy of residential communities.

Plans for residential developments can inadvertently undermine the emergence of a vibrant and connected community committed to their neighbourhood over the longer term. For instance in Manchester's city centre, low-rise blocks of flats are largely occupied by professional people, without children (LKA NI, 2008). This group of residents tends to be out at work during the day, returning late in the evening after work or possibly socialising.

Dwellings in residential areas that are left empty during the day and are not actively observed by neighbours are more vulnerable to crime (Rengert, 2015). In addition, opportunities to seek out help, if threatened, or for victims of crime to seek support are restricted by lack of social contact within the vicinity of the home. In view of the aging population, these are factors that may contribute to rising crime and impact of quality of life.

Services: design not machines

Automated systems are being introduced to perform tasks previously undertaken by service personnel. Unmanned petrol stations have been introduced, where customers fill up the car themselves and pay for it by inserting their credit card into a machine. As noted by the RAC – the UK automobile association – petrol stations are decreasing in numbers, largely due to fierce competition (http://www.racfoundation.org/uk-fuel-market-review/retail). The use of unmanned petrol stations can reduce costs and result in petrol stations being made available in rural locations that might otherwise be unprofitable. However, the absence of staff at petrol stations increases the risk of a range of crimes, including car theft, robbery and customer 'drive offs', where drivers intentionally leave without paying. Careful design can reduce crime and feelings of security, but not completely compensate for positive and responsive interaction with a member of staff.

The development of automated systems not only results in fewer staff to serve the customer but also increases vulnerability to crime and leaves the customer feeling unobserved or unprotected when faced with a difficult or threatening situation. Public transport systems routinely use ticket machines that are a focus for criminals, who attempt to break into the machines or target users for robbery or pickpocketing. The lack of staff in stations and on trains, metros and buses continues to deter people from using public transport. Better design of train and metro stations can contribute significantly to efforts to encourage use of public transport and promote more sustainable lifestyles (Smith & Cornish, 2006).

The use of automated systems is being adopted across a whole range of services: customer service staff are contacted via automated telephone systems;

airports expect passengers to check in, drop off baggage and proceed to security, all using a series of automated systems and machines; and supermarkets and newsagents have introduced self-service tills. In some instance, machines have led customers to commit theft because mistakes in payment are not picked up by the machine, encouraging active steps to avoid payment. Furthermore, customers frustrated by the self-service machines may feel little sense of guilt at not paying, even relishing the chance to 'get their own back' (Carter, 2014).

Mobile phone theft ratio

We have drawn attention to the role that product design plays in crime victimisation and noted that more could be done to make products less attractive to criminals. The factors that increase risk of crime and turn designs into 'hot products' have been clearly identified by Ronald V. Clarke (1999), and forecasting crime vulnerability is arguably not difficult. Importantly, mechanisms have been developed to encourage and support industry efforts to address security issues. Measurement mechanisms may be used to: (a) identify product brands and models vulnerable to crime; and (b) measure the impact of any security improvements that are introduced.

The mobile phone theft ratio was produced by the Behavioural Insights Team in consultation with the mobile phone industry. Published in September 2014, the mobile phone theft ratio provides consumers with information on the mobile phone handsets that are most likely to be targeted by thieves. Using crime data for the period August 2012 to January 2014, the ratio shows which phones were most stolen during this period, and details the factors which make a phone more likely to be targeted by thieves. The data can also be used to reveal emerging security problems. For example the data has already shown that 14- to 24-year-olds and women are the two groups most likely to be victims of mobile phone theft (Home Office, 2014).

We note that parents may be giving their children mobile phones in part for safety reasons, but inadvertently exposing them to crime and bullying. Likewise, women walking alone home at night may be talking on the phone to feel connected to friends and alleviate feelings of insecurity, but increasing their actual risk of being victims of robbery. Research is required to understand the vulnerabilities of these groups of users in these contexts, and the industry might be persuaded to develop safer smartphones and potentially other devices that meet their needs and requirements.

The mobile phone theft ratio highlights the success of new security features and sets out practical steps about how the public can protect their mobile phones from being stolen (Home Office, 2014). Apple currently has such a system built into iOS with Find My iPhone, an app and corresponding iCloud-based service that can remotely track, lock, disable and wipe an iPhone, iPad or iPod touch. With iOS 7, Find My iPhone was updated to include password protection and activation lock, the latter of which is an opt-in feature that provides users an added layer of security against stolen phones. When activation lock is switched on, nefarious users cannot turn off Find My iPhone, sign out of iCloud or erase and reactivate a given device without first entering the linked Apple ID and password. The idea is that a rendered-useless device ups the chances of recovery. In London, data on mobile phone theft demonstrated that theft of the iOS 7 quickly declined, as potential offenders found that the stolen smartphone was of no value to buyers of stolen products.

Technologies such as smartphones would ideally be designed to deter criminals from targeting the product. For firms seemingly unwilling to initiate steps to protect their customers, legislation might be introduced to support compliance with codes of practice. In the United States, the bill for the Smartphone Theft Prevention Act (as seen on US senator Amy Klobuchar's [D-MN] website) calls for smartphones to be equipped with technology that can wipe user data and render the device inoperable when stolen. If passed into law, the Smartphone Theft Prevention Act would require all phones sold in the United States to include kill switch–type technology free of charge. The burden would apparently fall on carriers to provide the solution, though how such a system would be deployed across a broad spectrum of devices was left unsaid.

We strongly believe that industry should act responsibly and that governments must take the lead in promoting and ensuring action within both the private and public sectors. To ensure wider benefits, product design and security could also be addressed on a European level.

CPTED theories and approaches

CPTED and related approaches are being applied to a wide range of issues, from terrorism, through crime and antisocial behaviour, to social problems, such as bullying, harassment and feelings of unsafety. Practitioners and academics are advocating more human-centred, holistic approaches to crime prevention that are suited to the particular context. In the case of bullying, for instance, the behaviour of all parties within the education context is considered – bullies, victims, teachers, parents and other children (who may encourage bullying or simply act as bystanders). The aim is to foster a climate at school and home where bullying is recognised and addressed, and where victims feel able to speak out (Brown *et al.*, 2011). It is also recognised that bullying of school pupils often occurs in locations that are more difficult for teachers to supervise – in the school toilets, during break time and on the way to school. Designers have an important role to play when it comes to 'socially engineering' behaviours that contribute to safety, security and quality of life for all groups.

A European standard for urban design and planning has not become compulsory. However, the process of developing a European standard enabled experts in the field to develop a common language, to identify and share good practice and to develop a standard approach in response to crime problems. This experience helps crime prevention experts to better support the design, planning and management of urban environments, and to continue to update their knowledge through networking with colleagues from across Europe (Grönlund *et al.*, 2014). In addition, government policies and legislation in some countries, such as France, are resulting in crime prevention being considered by designers in a more consistent way.

Efforts to develop guidance, training materials and case studies tailored to different stakeholders are ongoing. Key networks and organisations co-ordinating the production of knowledge include the European Forum for Urban Security (www.efus.eu), COST TU1203 (Crime Prevention Through Urban Design and Planning; http://costtu1203.eu), and the German Congress on Crime Prevention (http://www.gcocp.org). There is ongoing debate about issues, such as the implied 'rationality of offenders' and interest in emergent or more socially oriented approaches.

For all the design disciplines to contribute to the field, there is a need for networking opportunities concentrated around design and on leading-edge research to support design innovation. We have argued for crime prevention to be recognised as an important theme within socially responsible design, and have supported designers in their efforts to be at the forefront of innovation developments that meet multiple social and environmental objectives. However, further steps are required.

Design for the future

> 'Be humble in the face of facts, and proud in the face of opinions, as George Bernard Shaw once said.
>
> He didn't, actually. I just wanted to put some authority behind this observation of mine . . .'
>
> —Hugh Laurie (1996, p. 256)

Over the past two centuries, the methods and values of scientific thinking have vastly expanded our knowledge of ourselves, our planet and our place in the universe. Scientific thinking is arguably responsible for much of what we today would consider 'progress' – from the electric light to antibiotics to the Internet. Science is perhaps most closely associated with the concept of 'reason'. However, as well as the elevation of reason, we would suggest that in differentiating science from other systems of knowledge equally important is the elevation of empiricism. This resonates with good design, which has at its heart a similar belief in empiricism – in design it is called prototyping. And while the performance of design involves more qualitative and experiential issues, such as empathy and emotion, good designers must demonstrate equal humility before the facts. This is exemplified through the use of prototypes to understand users, discern problems, frame proposals and test solutions.

The role that design can play in helping address many of the complex human challenges facing modern societies is becoming more widely accepted (Design Council, 2015). Concepts such as green design, eco-design, social design,

design against crime, socially responsible design, transformation design and many more are now well recognised. We believe that the time is ripe for such design-led techniques to be seen as different 'flavours' of the same fundamental approach – the application of dynamic and creative human-centred design thinking, problem-solving and innovation to societal challenges. This broad approach is what we term 'Designamics'.

We are seeking to build an international nexus of sympathetic design researchers, practitioners and theorists with expertise in applying transformational design approaches to societal problems – including crime, feelings of insecurity and urban well-being. *Designamics* is envisaged as a 'virtual institute' of like-minded specialists in design – a collaborative network that shares practice, develops theory, shapes ambitious proposals and delivers innovative projects. If, like the authors, you're interested not just in design as commercial advantage but also in design as a dynamic of societal advance, we invite you to come join us (www.designamics.org).

References

Brown, E.C., Low, S., Smith, B.H. and Haggerty, K.P. (2011) 'Outcomes from a School-randomized Controlled Trial of Steps to Respect: A Bullying Prevention Program'. *School Psychology Review*, Vol. 40, No. 3, pp. 423–443. Download from: http://www.prevention action.org/what-works/school-wide-anti-bullying-program-really-works/5925

Carter, C. (2014) Shoppers steal billions through self service tills. *The Telegraph*. 29 January 2014. Download from: http://www.telegraph.co.uk/finance/personalfinance/house hold-bills/10603984/Shoppers-steal-billions-through-self-service-tills.html

Clarke, Ronald V. (1999) 'Hot Products: Understanding, Anticipating and Reducing the Demand for Stolen Goods'. Police Research Series, Paper 112. London: Home Office. Download from: http://www.popcenter.org/tools/risky_facilities/PDFs/Clarke_1999.pdf

Davey, C.L., Mackay, L. and Wootton, A.B. (2009) 'Designing Safe Residential Areas'. In R. Cooper, G. Evans and C. Boyko (eds.) *Designing Sustainable Cities*. Chichester, UK: Wiley-Blackwell, pp. 139–162. Download from: www.ndri.ir/Sites/Files/498/Design ing%20Sustainable%20Cities.pdf

Davey, C.L. and Wootton, A.B. (2014a) 'The Crime Prevention Capability Maturity Model'. International Perspectives of Crime Prevention 6. Contributions from the 7th Annual International Forum 2013 within the German Congress on Crime Prevention. Forum Verlag Godesberg Gmbh, Mönchengladbach, Germany. Download from: http://www.gcocp.org/kriminalpraevention/Module/Buecher/ISBN-978-3-942865-29-6.pdf

Davey, C.L. and Wootton, A.B. (2014b) 'Crime and the Urban Environment: The Implications for Wellbeing'. In R. Burton, R. Davies-Cooper and C. Cooper (eds.) *Wellbeing: A Complete Reference Guide*. Chichester, UK: Wiley-Blackwell, pp. 140–162.

Davey, C.L. and Wootton, A.B. (2015) 'Design for Security in Greater Manchester: Entwicklung eines Dienstes zur Integration von Kriminalitätsprävention in Urban Design und Stadtplanung'. In H. Floeting (ed.) *Sicherheit in der Stadt: Rahmenbedingungen, Praxisbeispiele, Internationale Erfahrungen*. Berlin, Germany: Deutsches Institut für Urbanistik (DIFU).

Design Council. (2015) 'The Design Economy Series: How Design Is Transforming the Way We Live Work and Play – Forever'. London: UK Design Council. Download from: http://www.designcouncil.org.uk/news-opinion/design-economy-series-how-design-transforming-way-we-live-work-and-play-forever

The Economist. (2014) 'The Backlash Against Big Data'. 20 April, by K.N.C. Download from: http://www.economist.com/blogs/economist-explains/2014/04/economist-explains-10

Finnegan, C. (2015) *Transforming Public Service Experience in Scotland.* London: Design Council. Download from: http://www.designcouncil.org.uk/news-opinion/transforming-public-service-experience-scotland (accessed 13.10.16).

Gehl, J. (2010) *Cities for People.* Washington, DC: Island Press.

Grönlund, B., Korthals Altes, H.J., van Soomeren, P. and Stummvoll, G.A. (2014) 'Review of CEN 14383. The Death and Life of Great European Standards and Manuals – Development and Implementation of the CEN 14383 Standards'. COST TU1203 Working Group 2. Download from: http://costtu1203.eu/wp-content/uploads/2014/10/03.-Review-of-CEN-14383-The-death-and-life-of-geat-European-standards-and-manuals.pdf

Harford, T. (2014) 'Big Data: Are We Making a Big Mistake?'. *Financial Times Magazine*, 28 March. Download from: http://www.ft.com/cms/s/2/21a6e7d8-b479–11e3-a09a-00144feabdc0.html

Home Office (2014) 'Crime and Policing News Update'. September 2014. London: UK Home Office. Download from: https://www.gov.uk/government/publications/crime-and-policing-news-update-september-2014/crime-and-policing-news-update-september-2014 (accessed 13.10.16).

Home Office (2014) 'Reducing Mobile Phone Theft and Improving Security. The Behavioural Insights Team'. London: UK Home Office. Download from: https://www.gov.uk/government/uploads/system/uploads/attachment_data/file/390901/HO_Mobile_theft_paper_Dec_14_WEB.PDF

Home Office. (2014) 'Alcohol: Government and National Union of Students Work to Reduce Binge Drinking at Universities'. *Home Office and The Rt Hon Norman Baker First*, 28 May. Download from: https://www.gov.uk/government/news/alcohol-government-and-national-union-of-students-work-to-reduce-binge-drinking-at-universities

Laurie, H. (1996) *The Gun Seller.* London: Heinemann.

LKA NI. (2008) 'Planning Urban Security'. Interim Report. Hannover, Germany: Landeskriminalamt Niedersachsen. Download from: http://www.lka.niedersachsen.de/praevention/vorbeugung_themen_und_tipps/staedtebau/staedtebau-152.html

Minton, A. (2006) 'The Privatisation of Public Space'. London: The Royal Institute of Chartered Surveyors. Download from: http://www.annaminton.com/privatepublicspace.pdf

Rengert, G.F. (2015) *Residential Burglary: How the Urban Environment and Our Lifestyles Play a Contributing Role.* Third edn. Springfield: Charles C. Thomas.

Smith, M.J. and Cornish, D.B. (2006) *Secure and Tranquil Travel: Preventing Crime and Disorder on Public Transport.* London: UCL Jill Dando Institute of Crime Science.

Stummvoll, G., Aquilué Junyent, I., Corbille, M.-A., Cardia, C., van Soomeren, P. and Galdon Clavell, G. (2014) 'Bellvitge: Unexpected Success – Against all Odds'. A Case Study on Crime Prevention by Urban Planning and Design COST-Action TU1203 Funded by the European Commission. Download from: http://costtu1203.eu/wp-content/uploads/2014/10/05.-Bellvitge-in-Barcelona-An-Unexpected-Success-Case-Study.pdf

Wakefield, J. (2013) 'Glasgow Wins "Smart City" Government Cash'. 25 January. Download from: http://www.bbc.com/news/technology-21180007

Wootton, A.B. and Davey, C.L. (2015) 'The Value of Design Research in Improving Crime Prevention Policy and Practice'. 11th European Academy of Design Conference Proceedings, Paris, 22 to 24 April. Download from: http://thevalueofdesignresearch.com

Index

Note: Page numbers in italics indicate figures and tables.

For Product Safety Concerns and Information please contact our EU
representative GPSR@taylorandfrancis.com
Taylor & Francis Verlag GmbH, Kaufingerstraße 24, 80331 München, Germany

www.ingramcontent.com/pod-product-compliance
Ingram Content Group UK Ltd.
Pitfield, Milton Keynes, MK11 3LW, UK
UKHW020947180425
457613UK00019B/568